Voodoo UNIX

Mastery Tips & Masterful Tricks

Voodoo UNIX

Mastery Tips & Masterful Tricks

Charlie Russel & Sharon Crawford

The Ventana Press Voodoo™ Series

Voodoo UNIX: Mastery Tips & Masterful Tricks
Copyright © 1994 by Charlie Russel & Sharon Crawford

The Ventana Press Voodoo™ Series

Library of Congress Cataloging-in-Publication Data
Russel, Charlie.
     Voodoo UNIX: Mastery Tips & Masterful Tricks /Charlie Russel & Sharon Crawford. -- 1st ed.
        p.   cm. -- (The Ventana Press voodoo series)
     Includes index.
     ISBN 1-56604-067-1
     1. UNIX (Computer file) I. Crawford, Sharon. II. Title. III. Series.
QA76.76.063R89 1994
005.4'3--dc20

                             94-8513
                             CIP

Book design: Marcia Webb
Cover design: Lynn Brofsky
Cover illustration: Mark Andresen
Technical review: Barry Nance
Indexer: Dianne Bertsch, Answers Plus
Editorial staff: Diana Merelman, Marion Laird, Pam Richardson
Production staff: Terri March, Dawne Sherman, Marcia Webb, Midgard Productions
Proofreader: Sue Versényi

First Edition 9 8 7 6 5 4 3 2 1
Printed in the United States of America

Ventana Press, Inc.
P.O. Box 2468
Chapel Hill, NC 27515
919/942-0220
FAX 919/942-1140

Limits of Liability and Disclaimer of Warranty

The authors and publisher of this book have used their best efforts in preparing the book and the programs contained in it. These efforts include the development, research and testing of the theories and programs to determine their effectiveness. The authors and publisher make no warranty of any kind, expressed or implied, with regard to these programs or the documentation contained in this book.

The authors and publisher shall not be liable in the event of incidental or consequential damages in connection with, or arising out of, the furnishing, performance or use of the programs, associated instructions and/or claims of productivity gains.

Trademarks

About the Authors

Charlie Russel has been geeking around with computers since 1985 when he went out to buy a loaf of bread and came home with a PC. At that time he was a respectable electrician, but soon was hooked on computers and now works in a big plant as one of those dread people you'll read about in this book, a System Adminstrator.

Back in 1985, Sharon was also an electrician, and although initially appalled by the computer, she quickly figured out that using it was a lot cleaner than repairing trains. So she became a technical reviewer, an editor and finally an author of computer books.

Charlie and Sharon have written several books together, including *Murphy's Laws of Windows*, *OS/2 for Windows Users*, and *Norton Desktop for Windows Instant Reference*. They live in Northern California with too many cats.

Acknowledgments

Lots of people helped with the making of this book, but none so much as the people at SCO (Santa Cruz Operation). In particular, I'd like to single out the following:

Elishiva (Eli) Steiner, my initial contact at SCO, and a wonderful person who provided me with software, support, contacts and encouragement.

Yasmin Kareshi, my primary support contact at SCO who *always* had the right answer and—always with great tact—helped dig me out of my own holes more times than I care to admit.

Dion Johnson and Tim Ruckles, Product Managers at SCO, who found the time to help out in spite of very busy schedules of their own.

Jean-Pierre Radley, Primary Sysop for the SCO Forum on CompuServe and a source of many tips and much help.

Dave Van Allen, Primary Library Sysop for the SCO Forum, who managed to have the files I needed, where I needed them, before I even knew I needed them.

Bob Stockler, Sysop on the SCO Forum, and the source for several tips that made it into this book.

Bill Campbell, a denizen of the SCO Forum, and maintainer of an excellent source of SCO binary and source files for anonymous ftp at ftp.celestial.com.

And, finally, the Santa Cruz Operation itself. All the people I came in contact with there were outstanding. No one ever shuffled me off to someone else or said, "Its not my job," even though I'm sure in some cases that must have been true. It says a lot about a company when the people who work for it are this good.

—*Charlie Russel*

Acknowledgments

In addition to all the splendid people mentioned by Charlie, I want to thank Elizabeth and Joe Woodman and all the other folks at Ventana Press who were such a pleasure to work with:

Editorial Manager, Pam Richardson, who is the soul of tact (and the eye of the storm); our very scrupulous editor, Marion Laird; and our technical reviewer, Barry Nance, who did his best to keep us honest.

Art & Production Manager Marcia Webb, who created an interesting book design; Dawne Sherman and Geoff Reiss, the capable desktop publishers; proofreader Sue Versényi; and Dianne Bertsch, who prepared the excellent index.

Last but not least, we thank Matt Wagner and the folks at Waterside Productions who handled all the paperwork and did a great job, too.

—Sharon Crawford

CONTENTS

Section II: UNIX Resources

Introduction

Maybe the title of this book, *Voodoo Unix*, strikes you as a redundancy. After all, if ever an operating system was mysterious on its face, it's UNIX. Despite its power and flexibility, UNIX has a reputation for being cryptic (deserved) and hard to use (mostly undeserved).

And because there are enough solemn and stuffy computer books out there already, we've chosen a writing style that's informal and just a bit impertinent.

Who Needs This Book?

This is a book for the UNIX user who wants to work better, faster and more efficiently. We've aimed our text at both experienced and novice users. Entries are short and to the point— no throat-clearing, no filler, just substance. You can pick up the book, read a paragraph, try it out and come away with something helpful.

We've collected tips and tricks of the trade that UNIX gurus use all the time—but you don't have to be a guru to master them.

Whether you're using UNIX because you love it or because it's your company's idea, you know that the UNIX universe is a vast one. Bigger than any one person can ever master. But even if complete mastery is not your aim (at least not right now), you'll find a lot in this book to like.

What You'll Learn

What we want to do in this book is to help you "grow" your UNIX knowledge. We try to show new ways to use some commands you probably already use, and add some new commands to your everyday repertoire. We hope you'll take what's here and use it as the kernel for stretching your skills. Because that's what UNIX is really all about. The more you use UNIX, the more skills you'll develop and discover.

How To Use This Book

This book doesn't have to be read in any particular order. You can read it from cover to cover if you like. But you can also look up a topic that interests you in the table of contents or check the excellent index. However you choose to use it, you'll find tips and tricks that'll help you subdue UNIX rather than the other way around. Every chapter also includes cautionary tales called "Traps" to help you avoid the pitfalls that await the unwary. We hope you'll always keep the book handy near your computer so you'll have an instant help reference when a problem arises in your work.

More About What's Inside

We've tried to organize this book in a reasonable way—sort of in the order you'd be learning UNIX if you were a newcomer. But you can use it in any order you like.

Chapter 1 gives you an introduction and an overview of UNIX, as well as all-important procedures for logging on and getting going. You'll find out about ways to set up your terminal and map keys to suit the way you work. You'll also find smart ways to pick a secure password and keep it private.

Chapter 2 shares shortcuts for navigating the UNIX file system and directory structures—how to name files, find strays and move around your directories with maximum efficiency.

Chapter 3 concentrates on **vi**, the fabulous, flexible (though just a bit intimidating) text editor that comes with virtually all versions of UNIX. You'll find lots of clever ways to make your text editing go faster.

Chapter 4, "Frogs into Princes," gives you good ideas for customizing your working environment. UNIX being, in general, a rather drab-looking environment, this chapter takes on the tasks of beautifying your computer while making it more efficient. Prompts and colors and other decorative arts are covered with handy shortcuts. If you have to switch from DOS to UNIX and back again, you'll particularly appreciate the section on making painless transitions.

Chapter 5 is all about printing. Printing can present a complex series of problems in a UNIX environment. This chapter gives you the information you need to produce your print jobs expeditiously. Because you're likely to be on a network, you'll also learn how to share a printer and not step on toes.

Chapter 6 is full of tips on running your programs in the most efficient manner. There are shortcuts and insights that can help you every day—such as how to run foreground and background operations and when to use both.

Chapter 7 has all the cool stuff about the graphical user interface X Windows. You'll learn about fonts, training your mouse and how to configure the X Windows environment to suit the way you work. This chapter also includes descriptions of many of the handy little (and not so little) programs that come with X Windows, and tips on which ones to ignore.

Chapter 8 takes you through the tools of your trade—tools that will make your life easier—in "The Magic UNIX Toolbox." You can turn to any page in this chapter and find secrets of the UNIX gurus that you can put to use at once. There are tools to help you navigate as well as manipulate files with ease. This chapter alone can double your arsenal of UNIX shortcuts and tricks.

Chapter 9 focuses on connecting to other computers. UNIX is the language of connectivity, and to get connected you need to know the magic words to send out in order to get replies. Chapter 9 also gives you useful information on network etiquette (or netiquette, as it's known).

Chapter 10 will show you how to avoid the UNIX mine fields that are waiting for the uninitiated. You'll see why UNIX can be not only a stimulating place to work but a dangerous one as well because it has no built-in security devices. This chapter gives you information that's hard to find anywhere else on keeping your UNIX environment safe. Included are ingenious and, best of all, *easy* ways to keep your work secure.

Chapter 11 moves you forward to a more advanced level. Here we take you into some of the structure and programming constructs of the Korn shell—including tidbits about **awk** and **perl**— that can make you look like an expert, streamline your tasks and impress others.

Other Stuff

At the back of the book, you'll find a useful Glossary of terms used throughout this book, plus other "UNIX-talk" you may come across in your travels. There are also *three* appendices for your computing pleasure:

* Appendix A   Command Reference: syntax and options for some powerful and interesting UNIX commands.
* Appendix B   Error Messages: Explanations of the UNIX error messages that are truly mystifying.
* Appendix C   Where To Go From Here: A resource guide to the best UNIX books and other places to get help.

Software Version

In its 25-year history, versions of UNIX have been produced by AT&T, Hewlett-Packard, Microsoft, Sun, Santa Cruz Operation (SCO) and the University of California at Berkeley, among others. In this book we don't dwell much on the different versions of UNIX. The commands and procedures we talk about are applicable to most old and new versions of UNIX—and when they're not, we make a point of it. Discrepancies that occur will be due to various versions of the UNIX shell—Korn, Bourne and C. As a user, it's more important for you to know what shell you're using than to be concerned about the differences among versions of the operating system.

Most of the examples in this book are taken from the 1988 version of the Korn shell (the most recent version). If you're not using the Korn shell, we think you should. Just type **ksh** and you're there. But if you want to stick with another shell, you'll still be able to use most of the examples and pick up a lot of useful information.

Your Favorite Trick

Most of the tricks, tips and traps used in this book came out of experience and luck (both good and bad). But because UNIX is made up of hundreds of commands that can be combined in millions of ways, we're sure there are some truly cool tips we don't know about. You can imagine how annoying *that* thought can be! So if you have a trick—whether it's neat and clean, down and dirty or sneaky and underhanded, we'd love to hear about it. If we include your tip in the next edition, we'll send you (in addition to a very polite thank-you note) a copy of the next edition free. So be sure to include your name and address when you write.

You can snail-mail to Ventana Press, P.O. Box 2468, Chapel Hill, NC 27515. Or better yet, send email to Charlie (crussel@netcom.com) or Sharon (CompuServe: 76216,1463). Actually, we'd love to get mail from you even if you don't have a tip, just to hear how you like the book.

Section I

THE MAGIC OF UNIX

 Getting a Grip on UNIX

To get a grip on UNIX, you might think the right place to start would be at the beginning—with installation instructions. Sorry, we're not going to do that. Installing UNIX is an arcane art form—best left to those who do it for a living. Each version of UNIX (and there are many of them) has its own peculiarities and quirks, and each version requires an intimate knowledge of the hardware and software of both the actual machine it's being installed on and any other machines that it may be connected to. In other words, it's the special job of that most holy of holies, the "Superuser" or System Administrator. This book is not written for them but for you, a person who works on a UNIX computer and wants to be better, faster and more efficient. But even if you're a beginner, you'll still find plenty of useful information here.

But what does (if you'll pardon the expression) make a UNIX computer unique? Most of us know pretty much what to expect from a DOS computer. It'll have one or two floppy drives, a keyboard, a monitor, an actual computer box and maybe a few other things. You sit down in front of it and start working. You can usually figure that you're the only person working on it while you're sitting there, even if you're connected to a network. Not so with UNIX.

With UNIX, you may be sitting at a simple terminal, not much more than a screen and a keyboard, with nothing but ugly text on the screen and apparently no computer anywhere around. Or you could be sitting in front of a beautiful, high-resolution graphics screen with a powerful workstation alongside your desk. Or it could be some combination of these setups. And in virtually all cases, there's a good likelihood that you're sharing the computer with other users. They may be in the same room or on the other side of the world.

So, with all those differences, how can you reasonably expect this or any other book to apply to you? Not to worry! Even though there're lots of differences in the different flavors of UNIX and the different machinery that it runs on, there are more similarities than differences. We will focus on those areas that are similar—where almost all the work is done anyway.

Demystifying UNIX

UNIX has a reputation for being an enigmatic, difficult and thoroughly nerdish operating system. And frankly there's some justice in that reputation. So why would anyone in their right mind want to use it? Because it's also a powerful, stable and remarkably flexible operating system, and once you know how to use its magic, it can be a productive and even friendly environment. Our goal here is to give you the tools and tricks to set *your* UNIX environment up the way you want it.

This book is not designed for the rank UNIX beginner. In most places, we assume at least a minimal familiarity with computers and with UNIX. We will deviate from that just a bit in this chapter, to make sure we are all on the same wavelength; so if this is all boring stuff, just bear with us a bit, or simply skip over what you already know.

A Little History Lesson

UNIX was developed at the Bell Labs starting in the late 1960s by many of the same people who created the C programming language (so now you know who to blame). In fact, they helped to drive and shape each other's design and implementation.

The idea was to create an operating system whose kernel (or core part) was as tiny as possible. The main driving force behind the small UNIX kernel was the fact that the developers were doing their work on what were, even by the standards of those days, tiny computers.

The first kernel was implemented on a tiny DEC PDP-7. Eventually they were able to obtain a new PDP-11 which had a total of 24k of RAM, of which the kernel took only 11k. This severe limitation on the amount of RAM resulted in a small, tight kernel with all the utilities implemented as separate, stand-alone programs. Each was itself tiny and designed to accept input from the preceding program as well as provide output to succeeding programs. A setup like this where the standard output from one program is accepted as the standard input for another is called *piping*. It's a powerful concept and is central to UNIX today. It has also influenced all the operating systems that have followed it.

Logging On & Getting Going

When you look at your UNIX terminal, you're presented with the login screen. This can be a cute graphical box with places for you to type in your user name and password, or a simple **login:**

In either case, type in your user name and press the Enter or Return key, whichever your system has. Next you'll enter your password, and we can get down to business.

Just a short aside here. Why, you might ask, should you have to go through this every single time you want to use the computer? Well, since UNIX is designed to be a multiuser operating system, it imposes certain security restrictions to protect you and your work from inadvertent or deliberate mischief. Payroll and other business records are good examples of the files that need to be protected by security measures. One of these security restrictions is that you must have an "account" on the system before you can use it. And, so that only you can use your account, you have to have a password as well.

When you first log in to a UNIX system, you will see a variety of miscellaneous stuff, most of which you don't care about at all. If you are at a text terminal, you will probably see a lengthy copyright notice go scrolling by, and a bunch of other stuff. Pay no attention. Finally, you may be asked what kind of terminal you're on. Chances are good you can just take whatever the default is, and get down to your business. But if you see a bunch of funny stuff on your screen, or the keyboard seems to be behaving peculiarly, it's a good bet that something got munged and the default is not going to be good enough.

Sometimes terminal type discrepancies won't show up immediately when you log on but only after running a particular program. In this case, it may well be that the program is resetting your terminal type, or that there's a problem that's less immediately obvious with the terminal type you're using. If it's a program that's resetting things, try adding the line shown in "Setting Your Terminal When You First Log In" to the end of the script file you use when you start up the offending program. If the program doesn't improve, get your System Administrator involved.

Setting Your Terminal When You First Log In

If your terminal isn't getting set properly when you first log in to the computer, it can be a pain. So, let's fix it. First, you need to know what kind of terminal you have. Sometimes this is easy— if you're at a Hewlett-Packard workstation, for example, chances are pretty good you have an "hp" terminal type. If you're using a personal computer and SCO UNIX, "ansi" is a good bet, and on a PC with a communications program to log into a remote system, your best bet is probably a "vt100." Almost every communications program will be able to emulate that. So, how to set it up? Easy. Just add the following line to your **.profile** (if you're running the Korn or the Bourne shell):

```
eval 'tset -m hp:\?hp -s -e -k -Q'
```

For those of you running C shell, it's a little trickier. Add the following to your **.login** file:

```
set noglob
set term=('tset -m hp:\?hp -s -e -k -Q')
unset noglob term
```

This, of course, assumes a default terminal type of "hp," which is nice if that's what you have. If your usual terminal type is something else, just substitute it for the "hp" above.

For more about the different shells in UNIX, see "Shells & Spells" later in this chapter. And for more about the **.profile** and **login** files and why you should care, see Chapter 4, "Frogs Into Princes" to find out how you can customize your working environment.

Tip **Want to see what your terminal settings are?** Often when you sit down to an unfamiliar terminal or workstation, you may not know what some of the settings are, so type this:

```
stty -a.
```

As you can see in Figure 1-1, this will give you more information about your current terminal settings than you are likely to ever want or need.

```
speed 9600 baud;   ispeed 9600 baud;   ospeed 9600 baud;
line = 0; intr = ^C; quit = ^\; erase = ^H; kill = ^U; eof = ^D;
eol = ^@;
swtch = ^@;susp = ^Z;start = ^Q;stop = ^S;
parenb -parodd cs8 -cstopb hupcl cread -clocal -loblk -ortsfl
-ctsflow -rtsflow
-ignbrk -brkint -ignpar -parmrk -inpck -istrip -inlcr -igncr
icrnl -iuclc
ixon -ixany -ixoff
isig icanon -xcase echo echoe echok -echonl -noflsh -iexten
-tostop -xclude
opost -olcuc onlcr -ocrnl -onocr -onlret -ofill -ofdel
-isscancode
```

Figure 1-1: *The impressive output from using the* **stty -a** *command.*

Setting Terminal Control Characters

The other terminal setting you probably want to do automatically every time you log on to the system is special-key assignments. These are set with the **stty** command. The following table shows you some of the standard control characters and what they mean. You can change these characters if you want. Many people, for example, map the kill key to Ctrl-X.

Special Terminal Characters

Name	Characters	What It Does
erase	Ctrl-H	Erases the previous character (Backspace).
kill	Ctrl-U	Erases or discards the current line.
eof	Ctrl-D	End of File - Ends the program or shell.
swtch	Ctrl-Z	Suspends the current program.
intr	Ctrl-C	Interrupts the current program or operation.
quit	Ctrl-\	Kills the current program, writing a core file.

To set these, use the **stty** command. Set just the ones you want to change or the ones you want to make absolutely sure are what you expect them to be. Then include the line in your **.profile** or **.login** file. We use the following:

```
stty erase "^H" intr "^C" kill "^U"
```

Tip 🎩 **Set the erase function to the Del key instead of Ctrl-H.** Type **stty** then a space, then erase, then a space, then Ctrl-V, then the key you want **Del**. However, the key combinations listed in the preceding table are by far the most common.

Tip 🎩 **Fixing your keyboard when you log in from a PC.** When you log in to your UNIX network from a PC, sometimes the version of **telnet** that's running on your PC doesn't remap the Backspace key properly. You'll think you have backspaced over a command, but when you press enter, you will find there are a bunch of control characters imbedded in your command. So, change the setting yourself. You type in the following keystrokes: **stty erase** followed by a space, then Ctrl-V, then the Backspace key, then the Enter key. The result onscreen will probably look like this: **stty erase ^?** Now the Backspace key

will behave normally. The Ctrl-V key combination causes
UNIX to read the next keystroke without performing
the action.

Tip **Put a little sanity back into your terminal.** What if
you got a little carried away with the **stty** command or, worse,
your terminal settings got seriously hosed by a *program* that
got carried away? To get back to reality, try the following: **stty
sane**. This command won't get your preferred settings back
but it will get rid of any truly bizarre settings. Exactly what
settings appear will vary depending on the system you're on,
but it'll be cleaned up enough so you can at least type characters into the terminal and see the results. From here, you can
reset things to the key combinations you prefer.

Shells & Spells

Many users think that what they see at the bare UNIX command line is the actual operating system, but it's really a command interpreter, called a *shell*. This shell is a program that sits
between the user and the underlying kernel of the operating
system. Its purpose is to protect the user from the kernel and,
perhaps even more important, to protect the kernel from the
user. In the MS-DOS world, this shell is called
COMMAND.COM, which is in turn often surrounded by
other shells such as DOSSHELL or the ultimate DOS shell,
Microsoft Windows.

In the UNIX world, you have a choice of shells. The oldest
of the shells currently in use is *"sh"* and is called the Bourne
shell. The Bourne shell is available on all UNIX systems. For
the interactive user, it lacks some critical features, such as job
control; but it provides a good base for writing most shell
programs.

Probably the most popular shell for the interactive user is *"csh,"* the C shell. Originally developed at the University of California at Berkeley as part of their UNIX implementation, it has many features for the interactive user, including the ability to recall commands previously used, as well as the ability to move jobs from the foreground to the background and back again (job control). As the name implies, it has a syntax and command structure that's modeled after the C programming language, making it particularly popular with programmers. Most versions of UNIX will have the C shell available.

Tip **If your command line begins with %, you're using the C shell.** The more worldly $ indicates the Korn or Bourne shell. A more recent addition to the shell game is *"ksh"*, the Korn shell. Named for its creator, David Korn, this shell is fully compatible with the Bourne shell but adds most of the features that made the C shell so popular, plus some completely new goodies. One of the most important of these is the ability to not merely recall an old command but to actually edit it. While the Korn shell is not available on some older versions of UNIX, it's becoming a standard part of most newer versions. In this book, we'll mostly be using the Korn shell, unless the C shell or Bourne shell is specified.

Tip **To tell which shell is your default shell, from the command line, type this:**

```
grep yourloginname /etc/passwd.
```

If that comes back with nothing, you are probably on a system that uses Sun's Network Information Service (NIS) to manage network-wide files. If so, try this:

```
ypcat passwd | grep yourloginname.
```

By one method or the other, you'll see the line in the system password file that controls your account. It will look something like Figure 1-2.

```
charlie:*:230:20:Charlie Russel:/users/charlie:/bin/ksh
```

Figure 1-2: *The line in the password file that controls your account.*

The various fields are separated by colons, with the last field showing the shell. The rest of the fields from the left are the login name; your password (this will either be encrypted or, as in this case, show only a "*" indicating that the password is stored in a separate file); your user id; your group id; a comment field which may contain such information as your real name and phone number; your home directory; and finally your default shell.

Setting & Protecting Your Password

When you log in, UNIX needs a way to know that you really are who you say you are. So, besides your login name, your account has a unique password associated with it. Your password is the most important protection you have against inadvertent or deliberate mischief which could cause you to lose files, or worse. Don't give your password to anyone, don't write it on your terminal or desk, and don't use anything obvious.

Yeah, yeah, we know. You've heard all that before. Well, let's try again. Protect your password at *least* as well as you would your VISA card. An unscrupulous person who learns your password can cause you an incredible amount of grief.

Here are some examples of bad passwords:

* Your login name
* Your name or nickname
* Your spouse's, child's or parent's name
* Your pet's name
* Your license plate
* Your Social Security number
* Any of the above spelled in reverse
* Common swear words or combinations of them
* "Wizard," "guru" or any similar sort of description

Rules for Good Passwords

In general, good passwords are those that can be easily remembered but don't lend themselves to being easily guessed. Here are some criteria for good passwords:

* Mixed uppercase and lowercase letters
* A pronounceable name
* Mixed alphabetic and nonalphabetic characters
* Six to eight characters in length
* A combination of characters that are easy and quick to type

An example might be something like "Moon4you." It uses two short words, with a number separating them. Another good example might be an acronym that is special to you, if it isn't something easily guessed—something like "OhiHacp" (Oh, how I hate all computer programmers).

Changing Your Password

You can easily change your own password at any time, and you should always do this immediately if you suspect that someone may know your old one. It's probably a good idea to change your password periodically, regardless. To change it, simply type this in:

```
passwd
```

You will be prompted first to enter your old password, then to type your new one. Finally you will be prompted to retype your new password. If the two don't match, you will need to start over.

Trap **Remember your new password.** If you forget it, you will have to get your System Administrator to give you a new one. The first time this happens, she or he will probably be fairly understanding. After the first time, the System Administrator will either be seriously annoyed with you or, worse, make fun of you unmercifully *in public*.

Trap **Check your new password immediately after you change it.** If you wait, and somehow mistype it twice, you won't be able to log in to your account. Inevitably, you will discover this only when you are in the midst of a crisis. So check it now, while you're logged in and have the chance to get it sorted out.

Trap **If you really need to write down your password, use some common sense.** Don't put it anywhere near your terminal or on your desk. Keep it in your wallet. Write it down somewhere you can find it but where it won't mean anything to someone who gets hold of it. And don't write the name of the computer or your login name in the same place where you write your password.

A Cry for Help!

UNIX comes with its own help system, and it's a good one. The entire UNIX manual set that takes up about a foot of your System Administrator's bookshelf is available online. For example, to get help on the **cp** command, simply type

```
man cp
```

which will give you several pages of information about the **cp** (copy) command. One of those pages is shown in Figure 1-3.

```
Name
      cp - copy files

Syntax

      cp file1 file2

      cp files directory

Description

      There are two ways to use the cp command. With the first
      way, file1 is copied to file2. Under no circumstance can
      file1 and file2 be identical. With the second way, directory
      is the location of a directory into which one or more files
      are copied. This directory must exist prior to the
      execution of the cp command.

      cp follows symbolic links given as arguments.

See also

      copy(C), chmod(C), cpio(C), ln(C), mv(C), rm(C)

Notes

      Special device files can be copied. If the file is a named
      pipe, then the data in the pipe is copied to a standard
      file. Similarly, if the file is a device, then the file is
```

Figure 1-3: *Help with the **cp** command.*

There are a couple of things to be aware of with the **man** command. It'll return the first entry in the online manual that matches the request, so if the command is one that appears in more than one of the manual volumes (usually numbered from one to eight), then you may not get quite the answer you are looking for. Usually this isn't a problem, since all the "normal" user commands are in the first volume of the manual set. If you know, however, that you need help from a particular volume, you can specify the volume on the command line. For example, a System Administrator might well want to know a bit more about the **passwd** command than an ordinary user would. But the extra information is in volume 1A of most manuals. So, to get that information, she or he would type

```
man 1A passwd
```

which would skip over the more limited help for the **passwd** command which is in section 1 of the manuals, and go directly to the manual entry in section 1A, which is written for System Administrators.

Tip **Some versions of UNIX let you get all the manual pages with a single command.** In SCO UNIX, for example, you can type: **man -a passwd** and get information on both the standard **passwd** command, and the extra help that's available to System Administrators. So check your system to see what switches you can add to the **man** command to make it work better for you. To do this, use the **man** command on itself!

```
man man
```

Tip **Getting help when only Divine intervention will do.**
Manuals, even online manuals, will get you only so far. Sometimes they just aren't enough. When all else fails, it's time to call your System Administrator. This mighty and all-powerful person, who also goes by the names "Superuser" and "root," is the one to go to when you have tried all other avenues of help, and you're desperate. This person has the power to give you a new password, or to log on to your account and fix things you have broken so totally that you can no longer log on to fix them yourself. She or he is generally the repository of a vast, though by no means limitless, storehouse of knowledge and tips about how your particular UNIX system works. But one word of caution. Like most gods, System Administrators are overworked and can be downright cranky if the proper offerings are not made. We suggest a large container of their favorite caffeinated beverage as a good starting point.

Moving On

This first chapter was meant to get you situated in the UNIX environment. Now that you know how to get logged in, tell what shell you're in, get help and set up a foolproof password, you should be ready to move on to the next chapter, where you'll find everything about smart file and directory management, including how to find the ones you've lost or misplaced, and where to find certain "standard" files.

2   File & Directory Incantations

Whole books have been written about the UNIX file system, so we won't even try to tell you all there is to know. What we will try for is everything you need to know to do your work faster and easier. Besides, a lot of what there is to know has little value to you unless you're one of those people whose job it is to tend the altar of the Sacred Server. So this chapter will help you learn to use UNIX in a way that will mean the most in your everyday tasks—to organize your work and find your way around the file system. There're also just enough shortcuts to make you look really smart if one of the UNIX gurus is watching.

Files & File Names

UNIX file names are much more flexible than, say, DOS file names. At the very least, they can be 14 characters long on the older systems, and these days most UNIX systems will support a file name as long as

```
reallyridiculouslylongandcomplex.file name
```

But that is probably not a really useful file name. The only hard-and-fast rule for file names is that they can include any character except a slash (/). Realistically, though, you should probably limit your file names to

* Alphanumeric characters
* Underscores
* Periods

Other characters may work on your version of UNIX, but they may not translate very well to other systems.

Files that have names beginning with a period are called "dot files." These files are hidden (actually, they're not completely hidden, but an ordinary **ls** command will not show them). You can "hide" directories the same way. In fact, many programs will create a raft of hidden files and directories in the hope that you'll leave these files alone.

Tip **Unhide those hidden files and directories.** Try the following, which works equally well with either the C or the Korn shell.

```
alias la="ls -aF"
```

Then use **la** instead of **ls**, and you will see all the files, including the hidden ones. The difference is shown in Figure 2-1.

```
$ ls
Mail
$ alias la="ls -aF"
$ la
./          .cshrc      .exrc       .login      .sh_history
.elm/       .kshrc      .profile    Mail/
```

Figure 2-1: *Showing the difference between what's shown with **ls** versus the more revealing **la**.*

As you can see, a lot more useful information is shown by the **la** command we just created than by the ordinary **ls** command. If your system supports it (and most do), you can change the -**aF** to -**AF** and get rid of the dot and dot-dot ("." and "..") from the listing.

Trap **What about the "/" after Mail and .elm?** Ah, that's a second little trick we snuck in to see if you're paying attention. The -**F** option to the **ls** command tells UNIX that you want to know the file type as well as the file name. If the file is executable, it gets an * after the name; if it's a symbolic link to another file, it gets an @ after the file name; if it's a directory, it gets the slash after it.

Tip **All UNIX file names and commands are case-sensitive.** You've probably already found out that **Charlie.txt** and **charlie.txt** are not the same file at all. However, it's probably not a good idea to get in the habit of distinguishing two files solely by a difference in capitalization. For one thing, if you regularly copy files from your UNIX system to other systems, like DOS or VMS machines, these two files will end up having the same name on the other system. For another thing, what makes you so sure *you'll* be able to remember which **Charlie.txt** is which? You can waste a lot of time opening the wrong files. So stick to the UNIX convention and use only lowercase characters for your file names, unless you have a particular need for an uppercase name.

Characters, Characters

UNIX lets you do things you really shouldn't do; this is one more example of its essentially programmer-oriented roots. The assumption is that you know what you're doing and really *mean* to do what you just did. Which is all well and good, but of course there's a potential for real problems when you don't understand all the possible consequences.

For example, DOS is pretty restrictive about what it'll allow you to include as an acceptable character in a file name. You're not allowed to create a file name with embedded spaces or weird unprintable characters. (Well, actually you can, but it is tricky and difficult, to say the least.) UNIX, on the other hand makes it easy to do this trick. But do you really *want* to have embedded spaces and weird characters in your file names? No, probably not. It just makes it a pain to copy, move, delete or otherwise do much with files that include such stuff, and it's by no means a foolproof way to protect them. So all it really does is make it a nuisance for you, while not providing any real security. Real file protection is discussed in "Protection Strategies" in Chapter 10.

Tip **Remove embedded spaces from a file name.** Just enclose the file name in quotes and replace the blank space with an underscore. For this we will use the **mv** command, which is UNIX for both move and rename.

```
mv "file name" file_name
```

Trap **The preceeding command will handle simple embedded spaces. But what if someone has managed to insert a weird character that isn't a space but looks like one to you?** Well, here's where we can use a wildcard to substitute for that weird character.

Tip **Use a wildcard to substitute for a weird character in a file name.** We'll talk more about wildcards shortly, but for now you can use a question mark (?) to substitute for any single character in a UNIX file name. So we could solve the problem above—a file name with an imbedded space—but this solution goes beyond the quote trick, since it works even if we don't know what character is buried in the file name.

```
mv file?name file_name
```

Well, that looks pretty good. But what happens if there are a whole bunch of them?

Tip **Use a simple shell script to change the name of a series of file names.** As most everyone who has used UNIX for any length of time has discovered, you can't use wildcards to **mv** a set of files to new names. Frustrating, isn't it? Heck, even lowly DOS lets you do *that*. Well, there are lots of ways to get there, including some really slick perl scripts. We'll touch on perl at the end of the book, in Chapter 11. But here's a simple little shell script (see Figure 2-2) that will automate the process of renaming a bunch of files, prompting you for a new name for each matching file.

```
#!/bin/sh
# Bourne shell script to rename files, interactively
for fname
do
        echo -n "Enter new name for '$fname':  "
        read newfname
        mv "$fname" "$newfname"
done
```

Figure 2-2: *A script to automate renaming of multiple files.*

A couple of notes here. The **-n** in the **echo** command line causes most versions of **echo** to suppress the new line that they would normally put at the end of the prompt. Putting single quotes around the original file name makes it clearer what file name you're talking about, especially when you expect to use this on file names that have embedded spaces. And, finally, you could just as easily use this script to *create* a file name with spaces in it, since the output file name is enclosed in quotes. So be careful.

Using Wildcards

Before you try your hand at wildcard tricks, let's review the rules. There are three basic wildcards:

* The ? character substitutes for any single character.

* The * character substitutes for zero or more characters.

* The notation [*charset*] substitutes for any single character in the set *charset*.

In order to understand this last wildcard, we'll digress for a moment to discuss what "sets" are:

A "set" consists of individual items that collectively form a defined group, or set. Any item that is within the group is referred to as an "element" of the set. And in UNIX we can define a set of characters by enclosing the individual characters inside brackets. So, to define the set of characters that might be used in the word "UNIX," for example, we would need both the uppercase and lowercase characters: U, N, I and X, since UNIX is case-sensitive, and someone might well type it as "unix," "Unix," or whatever. So we would use the bracket notation **[uUnNiIxX]** to define the set. The order here isn't important; what is important is that all eight characters be present, since each must be an element of the set.

This could get tiresome if one wanted, for example, to define the character set of all the lowercase characters of the alphabet. So UNIX provides a shortcut. The charset of all lowercase characters is defined [a-z]—that is, all the characters from a to z, inclusive. The set of all characters of the alphabet, both uppercase and lowercase, is defined [a-zA-Z]. Note that you don't add any extra characters inside the brackets (such as a comma to separate the characters from each other), because UNIX would just include any additional characters as part of the set. Finally, the set of all alphanumeric characters is [a-zA-Z0-9].

As you can see, UNIX supports a much richer and more flexible use of wildcards than DOS does. Which is why it's so particularly frustrating that some commands such as **cp** and **mv** don't support wildcards at all.

But in most ways, UNIX is far better with wildcards than DOS is. In DOS, everything after the * is ignored up to the period, so that the result of the following command might well *not* be exactly what you had in mind:

```
del *bak.*
```

Trap **Oops, you just deleted all the files in the current directory**—unless you were paying attention when DOS asked you to confirm it. Not so with UNIX. In UNIX, the * character substitutes for any number of characters, *including none*, but the rest of the pattern-matching in the line is respected. So *bak.* would match **newbak.save**, **oldbak.new** and even **bak.temp**, but would not match **newbak** because the trailing . (period) is missing. Well, that's pretty slick, and it does make life lots easier. You can even use multiple wildcards within a command, such as the following:

```
rm a*out*tmp?
```

to get rid of a bunch of temporary output files that looked something like **ab.out.tmp1**, **ac.out.tmp2**, and so forth. You can see how you can use multiple wildcards to make your life easier. But UNIX gives us another, even more useful option.

Tip

Use a wildcard set description to make your command line more intelligent. UNIX recognizes certain groups as being part of a set, and lets you use pattern-matching with that set. So, if you have a series of files, **file1.tmp**, **file2.tmp**, **file3.tmp**, **file9.tmp**, you can delete (remove) them with this command:

```
rm file[0-9].tmp
```

The best part of this trick is that you can remove only the ones you want. Let's say you make a "dump" (an export) of a highly important database every morning. You save the file to **dump.`date +%h%d`**, which yields a bunch of files called

```
dump.Jun23
dump.Jun24
dump.Jun25
dump.Jun26
```

and so forth. Let's also say the disk fills up pretty fast because each file is 100mb or so. So what you do is go in every few days and delete the old ones, leaving the most recent two. In the example above, you'd type the following:

```
rm -i du*[34]
```

This will remove all the files that start with **du** and also have either a 3 or a 4 at the end.

Oops, we did it again. What's that **-i** in there for?

Tip **Use the -i option when you're using the rm command around crucial files.** The **rm** is irrevocable and permanent. To protect yourself if you have critical, irreplaceable files, use the **rm -i**, which is the *interactive* remove command. This will prompt you for confirmation before any file is deleted. In fact, make it an alias and use it whenever you want to be sure:

```
alias del="rm -i"
```

You can even make this option the "normal" way **rm** is used; but you may quickly tire of being prompted every time you remove a file.

File Permissions & Protection

Since UNIX is a multiuser operating system, it assumes that you are not the only person who uses the computer. That's nice, and it makes some things much easier—like sharing files with your coworkers. But it also means that there are certain protections built into the system that allow you to control who sees, uses and manipulates the files you "own." Each user on a UNIX system has a unique user name and identification. Any files a user creates are owned by that user and can be read, used or changed only with the permission of that owner. A "long listing" of a file displays this set of permissions. For example, a long listing of the file **harold.cat** might look like Figure 2-3:

```
$ ls -1F
total 4
-rwxr-x--x  1 crussel users 884 Jan 30 14:47 harold.cat*
$
```

Figure 2-3: *A long listing of the file **harold.cat**.*

This says that the file is owned by crussel, who has permission to read, write and execute the file—the first **rwx** in the file listing. It also says that members of the same group ("users") have permission to read the file and execute it but may not change or write to it—the second **r-x** in the file listing. And finally it says that the world at large ("others") may execute the file but not read it or write to it—the third **-x** in the listing.

Tip 　**Use the chmod command to change a file's mode or permissions.** This command, which is short for "change mode," lets you easily change any file you own so that only those people you want can read it, change it or execute it. There are three basic levels of users, as we saw above: the owner (user) of the file, the owner's group, and everyone else (others); and there are three levels of permissions: read, write and execute. The three types of users are abbreviated "u" for user, "g" for the owner's group, and "o" or "a" for all those other people out there. The permissions are abbreviated the same as in the long listing above—"r" for read, "w" for write, and "x" for execute. So, to change the permission of the file "harold.cat" to allow users outside the in-group to read it, type in this:

```
chmod o+r harold.cat
```

The **chmod** command will let you make multiple changes to several files at once, so it is pretty easy to remove write permission from everyone and remove all permission from those not in your group for all the **.cat** files:

```
chmod a-w,o-rx *.cat
```

Tip 🎏 **Use the umask command to protect yourself automatically.** To protect files from accidental changes, add the following to your **.profile** (or **.login** if using C shell) file.

```
umask 022
```

Obviously, some explanation is in order. There are three sets of permissions for any given file. These are read, write and execute permissions for the owner, the owner's group and the world. We can think of these as three octal numbers, where full read/write/execute permission has a value of "7" ("111" in binary). To figure out what the **umask** command does, subtract the number for each set of **umask** permissions ("0" for user, "2" for group and "2" for world) from the default of "666," and you get "644" which means that the owner (that's you) can do what you want with the file but that others, whether in your group or the world at large, can read the file but not change it.

If the file is one that would normally be executable, such as the result of a compilation, the same mask of "022" will be subtracted from "777", leaving "755" readable and executable by the others in your group and the world as a whole; but only you have the ability to change it.

Tip 🎏 **Use umask to make life easier in a shared directory.** If you share files in a common directory, say on a project, you can make everyone's life easier by changing your **umask** setting to **002** whenever you are working in that directory. This way, new files created for the project can be shared and used by the others in your group. A sample alias for this would be

```
alias project='cd /users/common/→
    newmodel;umask 002'
```

Then, whenever you want to work on the new model project, you simply type **project** and you're on your way.

Tip **A quick pair of aliases to make setting your permissions easier.** Here's a quick trick to modify the permissions of a file, adding or subtracting write permission. Add these aliases to your **.kshrc** or **.cshrc** file, and they will always be there.

```
alias w-='chmod a-w $@'
alias w+="chmod u+w $@"
```

If you're a C shell user, this looks a little different, since the **alias** command has a slightly different syntax:

```
alias w- chmod a-w
alias w+ chmod u+w
```

But either way, we set these to *remove* permissions from everyone but add them back only for the owner. This is just good conservative practice. It's generally a bad idea to make global, irrevocable or far-reaching commands too easy to execute. Before you let everyone, even your boss, read your resume, you want to make sure it is on purpose. Speaking of which leads to another tip:

Trap **Nothing is secure from the Superuser.** It's important to understand this subtle but important point. You can set permissions such that no one but you can *even read* your secret file; you do this by setting it to a permission of "600" with the **chmod** command:

```
chmod 600 resume.doc
```

But this will only go so far. Even if we haven't accidentally left a back door into this file, by not setting the directory permissions correctly, *the Superuser can always read (and change) your files.* So think long and hard about what you leave on the hard disk. If something is really secret, a floppy is a far better place for it. Also remember that anyone who has your password has access to your files, just as if that person were you.

Directory Protections

There's more about directory structures later (see "UNIX File Systems & Directory Structures" below), but it's important here in the security section to mention how permissions work for directories. A directory in UNIX is simply another file name—for most purposes. It has the same set of permissions attached to it, except for the first column, which for most regular files is shown as a "-" in the first column:

```
-rwxr-x--x 1 crussel users 76884 Jan 30→
    14:47 alfie.cat
```

When the listing is a directory, however, the first column of a long listing will have the letter "d" in it, and the meaning of the permissions will be subtly different.

```
drwxrwxrwx  2 crussel users 4096 Jan 30 14:47 catstories
drwx------  2 crussel users 4096 Jan 24 06:52 Mail
drwxr-xr-x  2 crussel users 4096 Jan 30 14:48 voodoo
```

Figure 2-4: *Looking at the permissions for a directory listing.*

Here's what the permissions on a directory mean:

* read—permission to list the files in the directory.
* write—permission to create, rename or delete files in the directory.
* execute—permission to use the files in the directory or search for them with the **ls** command.

This means that even if you don't have permission to read a file, if you have permission to write to the directory in which the file resides, you can make a copy of it (which you will then own!), delete it, move it or rename it. And even if you can't read the contents of a directory or write to it, if you have execute permission you can still execute programs within the directory as long as you know (or can guess) the exact name of the program.

UNIX File Systems & Directory Structures

UNIX, like virtually all major operating systems, uses what is known as a hierarchical directory structure. This is sometimes also called a tree structure, but under either name it is the same basic structure as most operating systems these days. There's a "root" directory and under that root directory are a series of subdirectories. Each subdirectory can in turn have multiple subdirectories under it, which in turn can have multiple subdirectories under them, and so on. How deep this structure can go depends on the particular flavor of UNIX. But in virtually all cases, it goes far enough that you never need to worry about running out of levels.

So, what *is* a directory? Well, actually, it's really just a file that holds the names of the files and subdirectories that lie within it, along with the inode number for each file or directory. (Don't know what an inode is? See "Technical Stuff About Inodes That You Can Safely Ignore" below.)

Tip **UNIX has two special directory names that make moving around easier.** These are the . and .. directories, known as "dot" and "dot-dot." The dot directory is your current directory, while the dot-dot directory is the directory above where you are. So, if you are working on a project with a group of people and have your documentation files stored in one directory, your source code files in another, header files in a third, etc., it can be a pain to move to the documentation directory using an absolute path name. Do you really want to type **cd /usr/projects/newmodel/docs** every time you want to update the documentation on the change you just made to the header file, which is in **/usr/projects/newmodel/headers**? Hardly. So, to change to the documentation directory, just type: **cd ../docs**. Isn't that easier?

Technical Stuff About Inodes That You Can Safely Ignore.

The inode (pronounced "EYE-node") is the data structure that UNIX uses to keep track of where each file is in the system, as well as other important information, such as its permissions, ownership, timestamp, and so forth. In this sense, it's a little (but not very much) like the FAT table on a DOS disk. You can see the inode number associated with a file by using the **ls** command with the **-i** switch:

```
$ ls -il
total 4
441315 -rwxr-xr-x 1 crussel users 884→
  Jan 30 14:47 stanley.cat
```

So, what does this mean to you, as a user? Not much. After all, we did say you could ignore this section. This is the province of those shadowy figures known as System Administrators—the ones with pocket protectors and a persecuted expression on their faces.

The UNIX File Systems

The UNIX concept of file systems is somewhat different from what a typical DOS or even Macintosh user has come to expect. There's a "root" file system, which every UNIX machine must have, that is much like the "C:" drive on a DOS machine. But there the similarity ends. Instead of additional drive letters for each additional hard disk you add, the hard disks each get their own file system, which then "mounts" on the root file system. So, on a large system with many users and a substantial number of commercial programs on it, you might well have, for example, the root file system and a "**/u**" file system that contains the home directories for all the users, as well as another "**/usr**" file system that contains most of the commercial programs. And it's very possible even if you are working in a distributed workstation environment (as opposed to one with a large central server) that the **/u** file system is actually the same, whichever machine you happen to log in on. On one of the machines, it's physically in that box, but on all the rest, it is remotely mounted. This sort of setup allows you to use any available workstation. Your home directory is exactly the same, regardless of which one you use.

There's No Place Like Home

Every user on a UNIX computer has a home directory that is their very own. For user "charlie," this directory may be **/u/ charlie**, **/users/charlie**, **/home/charlie** or any one of several other places in the file system, depending on the flavor of UNIX and the biases of the Superuser on your system. But the result's the same. It's *yours*. Files and directories you create in it are owned by you and are seen, changed and used by others only with your permission (as always, with the caveat that nothing is hidden from the Superuser).

This home directory is where you'll store the files that control your environment and your startup files, and will also usually include a hopeless jumble of miscellaneous other files you've created over time. Sort of like the closet you throw everything into when company is coming. This makes it hard to figure out which file is which or find the one file you absolutely have to have right now. So, do a little organizing. Every user should have at least a couple of subdirectories to sort particular kinds of files into, and then use them. For example, my home directory has the following subdirectories:

* bin - Executable programs and scripts go here.
* docs - General purpose WordPerfect files go here.
* notes - A place for quick notes to myself.
* wrksheet - Spreadsheet files go here.
* source - Source files for various executable programs which are in bin.
* tmp - A place for temporary files.
* Mail - Required storage spot for **elm**, my mail reader.
* arc - A place to store compressed versions of things I don't often need but don't want to erase.
* junk - Stuff that doesn't fit anywhere else.

Other subdirectories come and go, depending on what projects are being worked on. For example, I currently have a voodoo directory in the docs directory. When this book is finished, the entire directory will get compressed into a single file and stuck in the arc directory.

So what actually gets left in the home directory? The absolute minimum possible. Everything that doesn't *have* to be in your home directory should be in a subdirectory. UNIX will run faster, because it has a positive dislike of directories with too many files in them. And you'll spend less time floundering around looking for files.

Tip **Keeping a lean-and-mean home directory.** Basically the only files in your home directory should be the "dot" files that control your startup, shutdown and environment. Files like **.profile, .kshrc, .login, .cshrc, .logout, .exrc, .xsession**. We'll examine most of these files in much greater detail in Chapter 4, "Frogs Into Princes," because they're essential to automating and controlling your setup. Since they begin with a dot, these files aren't normally seen because they're hidden from a simple **ls** command.

Finding Lost Files

The more work you do on a computer, the more files you accumulate. If you've created and are using subdirectories to organize your files, you've already made the first and most important step toward finding your files, since you won't be as likely to lose them in the first place. But sooner or later, you are going to lose a file. So, what to do about it? Well, there are some heavy-duty commands that can locate the file for you, if you know the file name. But there are also some simpler quick-and-dirty ways—the kind we all prefer, of course.

Tip **Use ls -t to find files you've changed recently.** This little trick all by itself will find 85 percent of the files you're looking for. The **-t** (for time, one assumes) will give you a listing of files sorted according to the time they were last changed, with the most recent first. Add the **-u** switch to this, and the sort is by time last accessed, whether they were changed or not. Combine this with **more** to prevent the listing from scrolling off your screen, and you have a useful alias:

```
alias lt="ls -laFtu | more"
```

This will give you a long listing of all the files that have been accessed recently in the current directory.

Tip Finding a file when you know what kind it is but not where it is. Now it's time to call in the heavy-hitter—the UNIX find command. This powerful utility will search your entire file system looking for a file or files that match a set of criteria. Or any subset of the entire file system. This is the command syntax you can use:

```
find <pathname-list> <operator>
```

where pathname-list can be one or more directories and their subdirectories, and operator can be any of the following:

*   name <file name pattern>
*   perm <file mode>
*   type <filetype>
*   user <username>
*   size <# blocks> (+# blocks means larger than)
*   atime <#days> (accessed time)
*   mtime <#days> (modified time)
*   ctime <#days> (changed time)
*   newer <file> (newer than the designated file)

Of these options, the most useful is probably the **-name** option. This will take wildcards and perform the usual sort of pattern-matching, so it can be pretty flexible.

For example, you know you have a file that you used for your monthly progress report last month. You want to use it as a template, but you can't find it. You do remember, however, that it had a file name with "Aug" in the name somewhere. No problem. Just use this command:

```
find ~/. -name "*Aug*" -print
```

In other words, find all the files with "Aug" in their name, starting from the top of the home directory tree, and print the result out to the screen. Note the use of quotes around the name. This prevents the shell from interpreting the wildcards before **find** has a chance to.

This is the most basic of find commands, and all other find commands come from this one.

Tip **Finding a file in a case-sensitive world.** If you aren't sure whether the report was "Aug" or "aug," you can easily add a second argument to the operator portion of the above command:

```
find ~/. -name "*Aug*" -o -name "*aug*"→
   -print
```

In this expression, we've used the "**-o**," which tells you to use a logical OR to do the search. Any file with either "Aug" OR "aug" in the name will satisfy the condition.

Tip **Use everything you know to find a file.** Sometimes you know several things about a file (except what you really want to know—namely, where it is). Let's say you worked on a file a couple of days ago, and that there are several other files on the system with similar names. In this case, you know two things about the file. To use both bits of information (part of the name and the fact it was worked on recently), type in the following:

```
find ~/. -mtime -4 \(-name "*Aug*" -o -name→
   "*aug*" \)-print
```

Here's the same logical OR expression but it's evaluated with the **-mtime** operator, now in a logical AND operation. So the whole expression means, "Find all the files that have been modified in the last three days *and* that have either "aug" or "Aug" in the name.

The combinations are virtually endless and the more you use **find** the more skillful you'll get with it. It doesn't always behave quite as you expect, however, so if you try something and it doesn't work, try breaking the command down piece by piece to see where *you* broke down. In the process, you will learn more and more tricks.

Shortcuts to Where You Want To Be

Moving around in UNIX can be a pain. Especially when you have long file names buried deep in a subdirectory tree. So, take advantage of the shortcuts that are available and make more of them.

If you have a directory you're using all the time, assign the path to that directory to a variable, and then export that variable so that it's always available. Make a simple alias to take advantage of the variable to move to it. For example, let's say you're working on a project with the new model group and you need to quickly move to the project's working directory:

```
/users/shared/projects/new/color
```

That's a real handful, and not something you want to type every time! So, try this:

```
PHOME=/users/shared/projects/new/color
export PHOME
alias goproj=cd $PHOME
```

Include this in your **.kshrc** file, and it will be available whenever you need it. The best part is, if you change to a different project, all you do is change the variable. Your fingers get to continue to use the same command.

Tip **Use cd all by itself to quickly return to your home directory.** This little trick will quickly get you back to your home directory, no matter how far away you have managed to stray.

Tip **Use ~ as a shortcut for your home directory.** When you want to describe a directory or file that can be found below your home directory, save yourself some typing by using "~" as a shorthand for your home directory. For example, to get to your personal **bin** directory from anywhere, type **cd ~/bin**.

Tip **Define a variable to describe any directory or file name you use a lot.** Shorten the long path name to any file or directory you use a lot, simply by substituting the variable in the command. Make sure you remember to export the variable, however, and include it in your **.kshrc** or **.cshrc** file. This way, it'll always be available.

Moving On

In this chapter, we've covered the most important navigational skills in UNIX. Now you know how to name, remove, find and classify your files as well as how to keep them safe. In the next chapter, we'll cover the vital matter of editing those files. And doing it in the slickest possible way.

3 Powers of Creation: Text Editors

Whatever your interaction with UNIX, sooner or later you'll need to edit a text file. And that's when you're faced with that most wonderful of text editors—**vi**. No, we're *not* being sarcastic. Originally created as part of Berkeley UNIX, **vi** is now included in virtually every implementation of UNIX. You can find other text editors such as **emacs** and **pico**. Of these, **emacs** is by far the more common, and it's on a lot of UNIX systems. But read this chapter before you go looking for an alternative to **vi**. We'll show you enough slick tricks and shortcuts to convince you that **vi** is not only efficient but fun too.

Using vi

Vi is short for "visual interface" and is actually an extension of the **ex** editor, which is itself an extended version of the **ed** editor. Almost no one uses **ed** anymore, so we can forget that, and the only people who generally use **ex** are those who are stuck on a terminal that won't support **vi**.

There are actually three versions of **vi** included in most implementations of UNIX. First is the standard one, which is mostly what we will talk about here, the one you start with the **vi** command. The second is a read-only version (useful for viewing files) that won't allow you to change files—either accidentally or on purpose. You run this version by typing **view** from the command line. And, finally, a version for neophytes that you start by typing **vedit** at the command line. This last one you can largely ignore. Some of the options included in the **vedit** version are pretty useful, but we show you how to add those to your standard **vi** below.

vi—Getting In, Getting Around, Getting Out

vi can be a scary thing the first time you see it. If you've avoided it before, here is the absolute minimum you need to know to get in, around and about and back out.

To start **vi,** just type **vi filename** and you will load the file into the **vi** buffer and be in command mode. From here, you can move around using the arrow keys on most terminals. Then, to insert text in front of the cursor, press **i** and you are in insert mode. Or to append text after the cursor, press **a.** To get back to command mode, press the Escape key. To delete characters, press **x** from command mode, and the character at the cursor will be deleted. To erase characters you have typed while still in insert mode, the Backspace key will work on most terminals. If not, it might be the Delete key on your terminal. Finally, to replace or overwrite text, press **R** from command mode and you will be in text replacement mode.

To save your work and exit, press **ZZ** from command mode. If you aren't sure what mode you are in, just press Escape a couple of times first. If you want to leave and not save your work because you think you may have mucked it up, press Escape and then **:q!** and you are out, with your file back to where you started.

Tip **Include all files you want to work with in the command line when you start vi.** You can use wildcards here, so it's simple to edit all your "dot cat" files by typing: **vi *.cat**.

You can get much more sophisticated, of course, using the pattern-matching built into the shell to load your files. But you get the idea. Once you have them all included on the command line, it's really easy to move between them in **vi**.

Tip **Use :n from command mode to finish editing the current file, save your changes and move to the next file in the file list.** This little trick saves you lots of time and makes it easy to edit a bunch of files. Just remember, if you want to cut and paste between files, you will need to use named buffers. See "Searching & Replacing" and "Cutting & Pasting" below for more on named buffers.

Tip **Use :e # from the command mode to return to editing the previous file.** The pound sign is a shortcut for "the previous file I had open."

Tip **To reload the current file and start again from scratch, use :e! % from the command line.** Here we are using external mode again, telling vi to edit a file without saving the current file (the ":e!" part), and that the file we want to edit is the current file (the "%" part).

Tip **To sound cool when talking to UNIX nerd types, the ! is pronounced "bang."** As in "e-bang."

Tip **Use the :args command to see what files are left to edit.** Loading a bunch of files on the command line is nice, but if you lose track of what's still lined up and waiting, this external command will show you what's left.

Tip **To start over on the same list of files, rewind them.** Use the **:rewind** command to save any changes to the current file, and start back at the beginning of the list or rewind-bang (**:rewind!**) to abandon any changes to the current file.

Modal Magic

Unlike most editors, **vi** is a *modal*, or mode-based editor. It has three basic modes: *command* mode, *insert* mode and *external* mode. In command mode, you give commands to the editor, such as "cut this line out of the text," or "save my work," or "move to line 37, and replace every occurrence of xxx with Ventana Press up to line 459." In insert mode, you simply type in text and it's inserted into your file. (Well, actually, into the buffer, but let's not be picky at this point.) And, finally, in external mode you are actually issuing commands to the **ex** editor or the shell directly.

In command mode, you can't just type text into the file. In insert mode, you can't just move down a page or over a word. And in external mode, you aren't really working with **vi** at all, but rather with **ex**. All this is just a bit different from most editors or word processors, and it can take some getting used to—okay, a lot of getting used to.

Trap **If you find yourself suddenly in ex instead of vi, simply type vi to return.** Chances are you accidentally pressed "Q" (that's the shifted Q key) which is the shortcut to go directly to **ex**.

Moving Around

The basic cursor movement keys in command mode are the "j", "k", "l" and "h" keys. They move you down a line, up a line, right one character and left one character, respectively. Add a number in front of them and you move that many lines or characters. So, to move 25 lines down in the current file, issue the command **25j**. However, if there are fewer than 25 lines below the current cursor position, **vi** will beep at you. The same applies if you're moving up and there are fewer lines than you specify. You won't get any movement until you supply a command that's possible.

Tip **To page through a document one screen at a time, use Ctrl-F to move forward one screen, Ctrl-B to move backward (up) one screen.** If you have a standard display with 24 lines per screen, this should be pretty good as is. However, if your display is some other number of lines, you can modify the behavior for an individual **vi** session by preceding either of these with a number telling the command how many lines to scroll. So if you type in 15 followed by Ctrl-B, your display will move up 15 lines.

Tip **To move the cursor a half-page at a time, use Ctrl-D to go down and Ctrl-U to go up.** Like the Ctrl-F/Ctrl-B pair, this can be preceded by a number to tell **vi** how many lines to move at a time.

Tip To move to the top of the file, press 1G (when in command mode, of course). This is a specific version of the general command G (for Go), which will move to the beginning of any line number in the file when the command is preceded by the appropriate number.

Tip To move to the bottom of the file, press G. There are lots of other movement commands, such as M to move to the line at the middle of the screen, H to move to the line at the top of the screen, and L to move to the line at the bottom of the screen. Don't try and remember them all. Just get used to using a couple of them that you can combine to get where you need to be, and you'll be fine. Don't forget that all of these commands are case-sensitive. If you should type in a lowercase letter instead of a capital, the results will be unexpected.

Tip To move to the beginning of the current line, press 0 (zero) or |. Zero is the shortcut. To move to another column other than the first one, use *n*| where *n* is the column you want to move to.

Tip To move to the end of the current line, press $. This one's worth remembering. You'll use it as you build some of the more interesting external commands.

Trap **Your screen may get seriously garbled.** If this happens, press Ctrl-L to force a redraw. This will usually fix the problem. But if this doesn't work or it seems to be happening a lot, you may need to ask your System Administrator to sort out the problem. It may have to do with a slightly off-terminal emulation. Which brings up a very important caveat.

Trap **Never depend on the "cursor" keys on your keyboard in vi.** Learn the basic movement keys, and use them. If you get in the habit of always using the cursor keys, sooner or later you will end up in trouble. You'll have to work on a different keyboard or you'll log into a remote machine that uses a different keyboard. The command keys are independent of the keyboard you're on, but that's not true of the keyboard's cursor keys, which may or may not be correctly mapped.

Tip **To see where you are in the current file, press Ctrl-G.** This will also give you a few other pieces of information, like whether the file has been modified since the last time you saved it. Another way to get this same information is the **:f** external mode command sequence.

Tip **To swap two characters, put the cursor on the second character, and type xp while in command mode.** This deletes the second character, then puts it in front of the first, which moved under the cursor.

Tip To change the case of a character, use the ~ (tilde) command. Like most **vi** commands, you can place a number, *n*, in front of this command to make it change the case of the next *n* characters.

Inserting & Replacing Text

Now that you know how to move around, you'll probably want to actually add something to the text. Here are the basic text insertion commands:

* ✶ i Insert text starting from in front of the current cursor until Escape is pressed.

* ✶ I Insert text starting at the beginning of the current line until Escape is pressed.

* ✶ a Insert text starting after the current cursor until Escape is pressed.

* ✶ A Insert text starting at the end of the current line until Escape is pressed.

* ✶ r Replace the character at the current cursor position.

* ✶ R Replace text starting from the current cursor position until Escape is pressed.

* ✶ o Open a new line below the current line. Enter will open another line, Escape returns to command mode.

* ✶ O Open a new line above the current line. Enter will open another line, Escape returns to command mode.

Almost all these text insertion commands work the same way. When you're in command mode, they'll switch you to text insertion mode and allow you to start entering text. The only difference among them is the specific location where the text will be entered. There is one command on the list that's slightly different: the **r** (lowercase "r") command, which will replace a single character and return immediately to command mode.

Tip **If you don't like the word you just entered, press Ctrl-W to retype it.** This is one of the few ways you can move the cursor position while staying in insertion mode.

Tip **If you want to start your text insertion all over, press Ctrl-U.** The other way to do this is to Escape back to command mode and press **u** for undo. The undo command is only a single level deep, though, so you must undo immediately or you'll have to fix it the hard way.

Tip **You can undo all the changes you've made to the current line by pressing U from command mode.** This gets around the single-level undo limitation, but only for the current line. Once you move your cursor off the line, you can't undo the changes on that line, unless they're still in the single-level undo buffer.

Most of the time, you have the text you want to replace right in front of you. This is where **vi** really starts to shine.

Tip **To replace the current character then insert more text without overwriting what's there, use the s command.** We know we can replace a single character with **r**, and we can insert text with **i** or **a**. But by using **s**, we get around the limitations of **r** without having to worry about overwriting something we don't want to. If you want to replace the next 10 characters then start inserting text, just type **10s** and start making your change.

Tip **To replace the entire current line, use S.** This will delete the current line, move the cursor to the first column and change to insert mode.

Tip **Use the c change command to change a word, a line or a sentence.** Actually, this command can do even more. Combine a simple **c** with a more complicated cursor movement command, and you can get really slick, as you'll see in the following table:

The Change Command

Command	Result
cw	Change text from current cursor to end of current word.
c*n*w	Change text from current cursor to end of *n*th word.
cb	Change text from beginning of current word to character in front of cursor.
c*n*b	Change text from beginning of *n*th previous word to character in front of cursor.
c)	Change text from current cursor to end of sentence.
c(	Change text from preceding start of sentence to character in front of cursor.
c}	Change text from current cursor to end of paragraph.
c{	Change text from preceding start of paragraph to character in front of cursor.
cf*c*	Change text from current cursor through first occurrence of character *c*.
c*n*f*c*	Change text from current cursor through *n*th occurrence of character *c*.
cF*c*	Change text from previous occurrence of character *c* through current cursor position.
c*n*F*c*	Change text from *n*th previous occurrence of character *c* through current cursor position.

On most versions of **vi**, the text you are about to change will be delimited by a **$** at the last character of the change. And in all cases, when you reach that last character, you'll change from writing over the existing text to pushing the existing text to the right in front of your cursor. This provides a powerful way to quickly fix a word, phrase or sentence then move on about your business.

The Dot Command Trick

Use the dot command (.) to repeat your last text change. This little trick saves bunches of time. Need to add a couple of spaces at the beginning of the next several lines? Well, you could figure out the exact command sequence and write a macro to do it (see "Macro Magic," later in this chapter), or you could just do an **I Escape** ("I", space, space, Escape) on the current line, press **j** to move down to the next line, then press . (dot). Do this for each line you need to indent.

Searching for Text

OK, that's nice, but how about just finding some text? Ah, now we get into external mode. Here we use the **ex** command set. So, here's how to search from the current cursor position for something we use:

    /searchpattern

To search backward, we use this:

    ?searchpattern

The search pattern can be a simple bit of text, like searching for the word "Priscilla" in a file, or it can be a more complicated pattern-matching string. But let's save the pattern matching discussion for just a moment.

Searching & Replacing

Finally, what we've all been waiting for—search and replace! After all, any editor worth its salt will let you do that, right? Otherwise you are going to have to go through and manually change all those references to your boss. And what happens if you miss one? Doesn't bear thinking about.

Tip **To search for a pattern and replace it with another, use the external mode substitute command.** The syntax is

`x,ys/searchpattern/replace/options`

where *x,y* are the beginning and end of the search-and-replace zone, and *options* include **g** for "globally do it and don't bother asking me," and **c** for "ask me to confirm each change."

So, here's how to find all those unflattering references to your boss and replace them with Priscilla:

`1,$s/catbrain/Priscilla/g`

As a substitute for the **1,$** of this command, you can use **%**, if saving the two keystrokes is important enough to you to bother remembering it.

Tip **You don't have to know what line you're on to run substitute on the next ten lines.** Use the . (dot) to represent the current line, and then tell **vi** to do the substitution for the next 10 lines:

`.,+10s/fishbreath/Alfie/g`

To make sure you don't accidentally change something you didn't mean to, use the **c** option after the final slash. This will print the string to be substituted with "^" characters highlighting it. Press "Y" to make the change, press anything else to leave it as is.

Tip

77 To execute a command on an entire file, use the global command. This command lets you search through a file and execute the yank command, for example, to append the lines that match a particular pattern to a buffer. Thus,

```
:g/Priscilla/y A
```

will grab all those lines with "Priscilla" in them, place them in buffer a, appending them after anything already there. This command lets you do some fairly tricky things, such as search for all lines that begin with a number, and indent them five spaces:

```
:g/^[0-9]/s/^/     /g
```

Using this command, the text in Figure 3-1 becomes lined up like the text in Figure 3-2.

```
Widget Sales Report
1. Sumatra
2. Shanghai
3. Senegal
4. Cincinnati
Climatic impact on widget sales
Widgets in the EcoSystem
~
~
~
~
~
```

Figure 3-1: *Text before a global rearrange command.*

```
Widget Sales Report
     1. Sumatra
     2. Shanghai
     3. Senegal
     4. Cincinnati
Climatic impact on widget sales
Widgets in the EcoSystem
~
~
~
~
~
```

Figure 3-2: _After the global command, the numbered lines are indented._

Let's examine this little bit of magic more closely. Here's what the command means, piece by piece:

Command	Result
:	do this command in **ex** mode
g	execute the global command
/^[0-9]/	search for lines that begin (the ^) with a number
s	execute the substitute command
/^/ /g	substitute 5 spaces (or put the number of spaces you want between the last two slashes) for the beginning of the line, and do it globally without asking.

As you can see, this command gives us some pretty powerful ways to manipulate text within **vi**, using the external mode commands.

Cutting & Pasting

To cut a line into the paste buffer, press **dd**. This will cut a single line of text. Oh, you wanted the next 10 lines? Simple— **10dd** and you have them.

To copy a line into the paste buffer, press **yy** (the "yank" command). This works just like **dd** except that the line or lines are copied to the buffer, not deleted.

To cut a character, use the **x** command. This will delete the character under the cursor, pulling the line back. When it reaches the end of the line, it starts deleting the character before the cursor (backspace). For 10 characters, use **10x**.

Trap **Text in the paste buffer is only a single level.** As soon as you make a deletion or "yank" (copy) to the paste buffer, you lose what was in there before. So, think before you yank or delete something. Have you finished with the current buffer's contents?

Deleted Text

Deleted (cut) text goes into a buffer "stack," so using the **dd** command is better than yanking. This is a neat little trick that even a lot of **vi** gurus don't know. If you yank text, it doesn't go into the stack, so you can only get at the last text you yanked. But if you delete it, it goes into a 9-level "stack" (last in, first out). So, to add a line to the stack, without actually deleting it, do a **dd** followed immediately by **P**. Your file hasn't changed, but you have added the current line to the buffer. Now, go ahead and delete something else. Want that first line back? It has now been pushed up one level on the stack by the second deletion, so to get it back, do a **"2p** and you will insert it after the current line. Pretty slick. The only problem with this, however, is keeping track of what's in which buffer. Using named buffers is better, because they don't change unless you overwrite them. But if you get in the habit of using the **ddP** combination instead of **yy**, you will save yourself some grief often enough to make the extra keystroke worth it.

Tip **Use the named buffers to keep text pieces handy.** All that deleting and yanking is nice, but what if you need to grab a piece from here, a piece from there, and another piece from somewhere else? Hmmm, that single level buffer isn't going to get it done, is it? No sweat—vi provides for a total of 26 "named buffers." That should be enough for almost anyone. The buffers are named a-z. You cut or copy text into them in exactly the same way you would into the regular cut/copy/paste buffer—except you precede the cut or copy command (dd or yy) with "a for the a buffer, "b for the b buffer, etc.

Tip **To put the contents of the paste buffer after the current line, use the p command.** If you have cut or yanked only a partial line, the text in the buffer will be placed in the current line, after the current cursor position. Use **P** to place the text before the current line or position.

Tip **Use named buffers for your paste operation by preceding the paste command with "a where a is the named buffer.** If the text you want is in the b buffer, use **"b**, and so forth.

Tip **To cut a word into the buffer, use dw.** Actually, this is the simplest example of the more general rule. Use d*cursormovement* or y*cursormovement* to cut or copy text into the buffer. The cursor movement keys are the same as for the change command of the first table in this chapter.

Getting the Right Look

Choosing and using an editor is a very personal thing. One that works well for some people may not work well for others. So, a good editor lets the user change the way it behaves and looks, to make it more comfortable for that particular user. In **vi,** there are three basic commands to change the look and feel, and they're all external mode commands. The first command is the **:set** command. Use this to set all sorts of options. The list may vary slightly, depending on your particular implementation of **vi**, but here are some of the most common:

vi Options

Option	Description
ai	autoindent - New lines start lined up with the indent from the previous line.
noai	autoindent off (the default)
aw	autowrite - Current buffer contents are written when escaping to the shell, or using :n to go to the next file.
noaw	autowrite off (the default)
flash	Flash screen on an error instead of beeping (the default).
noflash	Use a beep instead of a flash.
ic	Ignore case on searches or pattern-matching..
noic	Don't ignore case (the default).
lisp	Set autoindent to line up better when editing lisp programs.
nolisp	Align autoindent lines with the beginning of previous line (the default).
magic	Use the full set of metacharacters when doing pattern matching (the default).
nomagic	Limit metacharacters to only ^ and $.
mesg	Allow other users to write to your terminal (the default).
nomesg	Disable write permission to the screen.
nu	Display line numbers along the left edge of the screen.
nonu	Do not display line numbers (the default).
ro	Make file read-only (to prevent the file from being changed without explicitly overriding the setting with :w!).
noro	Make file normal read/write mode (the default).
remap	Allow macro definitions to link directly to already mapped commands (the default).
noremap	Cause macro definitions to be explicit.

vi Options, continued

Option	Description
showmatch	Highlight matching { or (briefly when a closing) or } is typed.
noshowmatch	No highlighting of matching delimiters (the default).
showmode	Show a highlighted mode indicator on bottom line when in text entry mode.
noshowmode	Don't indicate the current mode (the default).
ts=n	Set tab spacing to n characters. Default is 8.
warn	Warn before a shell escape when text has been modified since the last write command (the default).
nowarn	Don't warn before shell escapes, just do it.
ws	Wrap searches around to the beginning of the file and keep going (the default).
nows	Don't wrap when the end of the file is reached in a search.
wm=n	wrapmargin - When set to other than zero, automatically insert a new line when the current word would exceed the margin. The number of characters from the right hand edge of the display for the margin—i.e., wm=8— sets the right margin on an 80-column display at column 72.

Tip

Set showmode to on. It's a nuisance to suddenly find you are inserting text, just because you accidentally hit the wrong key. This simple little change gets over that, giving you a gentle reminder whenever you are in text insertion mode. Just type **:set showmode** to set this on.

Tip

Use autoindent when you are writing shell scripts or program code to make your files easier to read. This way, when you write if or case statements, or other programming structures, it's easier to set them off so that they are clear.

Tip

Use showmatch to help find matching braces when you are writing programming code. This can make it much easier to tell which brace or bracket you are closing, since the cursor will jump to the corresponding opening brace or bracket for a second, then back. This can be a minor annoyance when you're just typing a letter, not writing code. So, turn it off with **:set noshowmode**.

Tip

Put all your "normal" settings in the file .exrc in your home directory. This file is automatically loaded every time you start **vi** unless there is a file of the same name in your current directory.

Tip

If you have different settings for different tasks in vi, create directory-specific .exrc files for each task. If you use **vi** to write notes as you work on things and you keep all these notes in the same directory, it's easy to set up a special **.exrc** file for that directory that's more appropriate for note-taking. Set **wrapmargin=8** for this directory, for example. While your shell script directory gets a **.exrc** with wrapmargin off and auto-indent on.

Tip

Use comments in your .exrc file to make it easier to understand. Any line that begins with a double quote mark(") is ignored by **vi** when it starts. It may take a moment longer to start up, but it's a lot easier to remember why you have a certain option set if you put a comment in the file. And as we will see with mappings in the section "Macro Magic" below, this really becomes important there.

The **.exrc** file's format is exactly the same as the format you'd have when entering the commands inside **vi** while in command mode. So, it might look something like Figure 3-3.

```
:set ai
:set ts=5
:set wm=5
:set showmode
:set showmatch
:set nonu
"Now some simple mappings to make the book easier.
:map ; :
" Map F7 to search for vvdu and substitute the book title
:map  #A ^[1,$s/vvdu/Voodoo UNIX/g ^M
" Map! F7 in insert mode to place " vvdu " in the text at the
" current cursor position. The extra spaces have to be escaped
" with ^V to enter them, or vi ignores them.
:map! #A  vvdu
"And an abbreviation, cause I'm lazy
:abbr ux UNIX
```

Figure 3-3: *Using comments as reminders in your* **.exrc** *file.*

Macro Magic

Macros give you a way to automate frequently used command sequences, and shorten the number of keystrokes it takes to do the things you do all the time. Plus it's a lot easier to remember that you use Ctrl-F1 to run UNIX's spell checker and put a list of the misspelled words at the bottom of the current file than to remember and type in the command every time. **Vi** has three different kinds of macros: the **:map** command, which runs a series of keystrokes from the command mode: the **:map!** command, which does the same thing when you start in text insertion mode; and the **:abbr** command, which lets you abbreviate frequently used words or expressions and have them automatically expanded by **vi** as you type them in text-insertion mode. You can enter these commands directly in **vi** when you are in command mode, or you can include them in your **.exrc** file. We find it helps to have different sets of these for each project, and include them in a separate **.exrc** file in each project's main directory.

Tip

Use the :map command to automate frequently used sequences that start in command mode. This is the syntax:

```
:map key replacement
```

The key can be almost any key on the keyboard, but if it's a function key or control key, you will have to "escape" its meaning by first entering a Ctrl-V. So, for example, to map Ctrl-F1 to run UNIX's spell checker, and put the results at the bottom of the current buffer (file), the command is:

```
:map #^ G:w!^M:r !spell %^M
```

The Enter keys in this sequence would cause the map to terminate, so you must use the key sequence "Ctrl-V,Ctrl-F1,space,G:w!,Ctrl-V,Enter,:r,space,!spell,space,%,Ctrl-V,Enter". The Enter keys have to be "escaped" with Ctrl-V first. They appear in the command as ^M or Ctrl-M, which is what the Enter key actually is, of course. So, what does this command do? First it moves to the bottom of the buffer, the "G", then it writes out the current contents of the buffer to the disk file unconditionally, the ":w! Enter". Then, it reads *into* the buffer the result of running the spell command on the current file, the ":r !spell %Enter".

The total number of **:map** and **:map!** commands you can define at any one time are 32 for most versions of **vi**, and they can be no more than 512 characters total. This should be more than enough for almost all purposes, especially if you separate them into separate **.exrc** files for each task, which makes the most sense.

Tip Use the "map bang" macros to automate frequent tasks that start while in text insertion mode. For example, if you are the sort of person who likes to save your current work frequently (not a bad idea, though **vi** will usually be able to recover even if you do crash or have a power failure), here's a simple macro to save your current work and continue without losing your place in the file.

```
:map! #= ^[:w!^Ma
```

This command, which is mapped on the F3 key, begins with an escape to take you to command mode, then the ":w!Enter" sequence to write the current file out to disk, and finally an "a" to take you back into text insertion mode right where you left off. Note that both the "Escape" key and the "Enter" key must be escaped with Ctrl-V or they will be misinterpreted.

Tip Use the map! command to make a text insertion mode command that behaves like the Ctrl-G of command mode to see where you are in the current file. This one is handy if you just want to know where you are in the file without having to go out to command mode and come back. Well, actually you do have to go out and back, but it's all automatic:

```
:map! ^G ^[^V^Ga
```

Trap But this one's a little tricky. Because Ctrl-G has a special meaning, you can't just enter it. And if you enter a single Ctrl-V, it will simply escape what you are trying to do. So, the trick to this one is that the first Ctrl-G must be entered with a Ctrl-V,Ctrl-G sequence, then Ctrl-V, Escape,Ctrl-V,Ctrl-V,Ctrl-G, and a final "a" to go back into text insertion mode.

> **Tip** **Use :abbr to reduce the number of keystrokes you need to enter for common phrases.** This one is so simple you should do it on the fly whenever you find yourself repeatedly using the same sequence. And it's handy for creating standard phrases so that an entire workgroup uses the same wording for critical phrases. For example, while writing this chapter we must have used the sequence **<cd>vi<bt>** a zillion times, since we wanted it to appear in "program text" not in regular text. Well, that got awfully old real quick. So, we added the following abbreviation to our **.exrc** file: **:abbr vvi <cd>vi<bt>**.

As you type along, abbreviations are automatically expanded to their full meaning as you go, unlike some word processors that wait until you tell them to expand the abbreviations.

Reading, Writing & 'Rithmetic

Whatever you do with **vi,** you'll need to save your work when you're finished. And you'll often need to be able to read in other files or text, and even get some simple statistics on that Great American Novel you are writing in **vi.** The commands to write out your work, read other files in, and quit are mostly external mode commands that start with ":". Though there are some "shortcuts" that work in command mode. To save your work and quit, you can use the command mode sequence **ZZ** or the external mode sequence **:wq**. We find the **:wq** more intuitive and easier to type—but to each their own. And if you want to create a series of function key mappings to do this, feel free. Charlie spent so much time with WordPerfect that he has his F7 key mapped to do this **:map ^[[S :wq!^M**; Sharon has hers mapped to Alt-F4.

Tip **To include another file in your current file, use the :r (read) command.** This is handy if for example you want to include some standard header text that's too big a block to put in a map or abbreviation.

Scratch File

To write out part of your current file to a "scratch" file, tell the write command how much and where. To write the whole current file back out, we use the short form of the write command :**w**. But to write out the next 10 lines, including the current one, to a file called "junk," use the longer form of write:

```
:.,+10w junk
```

This will write out the current line and the next 10 lines to the file named junk.

Tip **When you are sure you have done something horrible to your file, use "quit-bang" to quit without saving.** That's :**q!** and it always gets you out.

Tip **Finally, the "smart" exit command.** Use :**x** if you want to save the current file if it has changed or leave it unchanged if you haven't modified it, and, either way, exit back to your shell. This should probably be your "normal" exit command, unless you want the file's date and time to be updated when you exit without having made any changes.

Arithmetic

Use UNIX's built-in word count program to get some information about your file. We promised some arithmetic in the heading for this section, so here it is. You can send your file through the **wc** word count utility to find out how many words or lines are in your file. It will even give you a total for all the files in the list you give it. To get a total word, line and byte count for the seven dot-cat files in our /save directory, we get this:

```
$ wc -lwc *.cat
      14      84      573 alfie.cat
     140     790     6346 guz.cat
     280    1580    12692 harold.cat
      56     311     2600 meep.cat
      70     395     3173 possm.cat
     266    1496    12119 pris.cat
     560    3160    25384 stanley.cat
    1386    7816    62887 total
```

This shows us that we have a total of 1,386 lines, 7,816 words, and some 62,887 bytes of text in the seven files.

Trap **If your system crashes before you have written your changes, use the recover command.** If you end up exiting from **vi** because something causes your system to crash, you can almost always recover what you were working on, using the special **vi -r** *filename* command. Then save the file back out, just in case.

The Other Editor—Emacs

Well, there are other editors out there in the UNIX world if you just can't stand the thought of **vi**. Personally, we think you are making a mistake, but it's your call. Of the generally available ones out there, the most widely available one is certainly **emacs**, which is short for "editor macros." Unlike **vi**, it's a more traditional editor, not a modal editor. What you type generally goes into the file, and when you want to do something other than just enter text, you use Control key or keys to tell **emacs** you want it to do something special. And **emacs** can do a lot of special things. It's a powerful package that can do all the things **vi** can do and lots more, if you care to teach it those extra things.

To extend **emacs**, you really need to be a Lisp programmer, since **emacs** is a lisp-based program. But, don't let that frighten you. You can make a very good start indeed by just borrowing some of the things your friends have done, and tweaking them for yourself. Plus some things, like building macros and abbreviations, are already there and ready to go. So, if you want to give **emacs** a try, and you don't have a copy on your system, ask your System Administrator to see about getting a copy.

There are also other editors to be found, and many of them are available for the price of a download. In addition, friendly, easy-to-use commercial graphical-based editors are now available for those of you running under Xwindows. But you won't find many, if any, that are as powerful as either **vi** or **emacs**.

Moving On

We've covered all sorts of tricks with our favorite editor, **vi**, and shown you how to use it and customize it. So now you can use **vi** (or some other text editor, if you absolutely insist) to edit some of the basic files that control your everyday work environment. Next, we'll move on to transforming your UNIX environment into a place that's not only nice to visit but a nice place to live as well.

4 Frogs Into Princes

Everyone's different, right? So your UNIX environment can be different from someone else's as well. The System Administrator can, and should, set up a reasonable starting point for you, but after that, it's up to you. Decisions about your work space can be as simple as changing the color of your screen and desktop in X Windows, or as far-reaching as deciding on a particular shell to run.

Some people go for the "messy desk" approach, with all sorts of add-ons, files and neat little goodies to make their lives a bit better, while others go for the lean-and-mean approach. Most of us fall somewhere in between. We're not going to tell you how you should set your environment up. That's much too personal a decision. But what we will do is show you some tips and tricks that can make your life with UNIX easier and more productive. You choose the ones that make sense for you, and we will try to point you in the direction of finding and implementing even more changes to suit yourself.

The process has already started, in the previous chapter when we showed you how to create a **.exrc** file for your home directory where you can store your default **vi** setup. But now we'll take a look at some other changes you can make.

Startup Script Magic

The single most important change you'll make to your work environment is in your startup scripts. Depending on the shell you use, this may involve only a single file, or you may use several.

For the most part, though, you'll have two very important files to worry about if you're in text mode; you'll have one or more additional ones if you're running in X Windows or some derivative of X Windows, such as HPVue or SCO Open Desktop. We can't get into the specifics of each X Windows shell in this book, but we'll deal with some of the more general things you can do. Then you can use the documentation you received with your system, plus what you learn here, to tweak HPVue, or whatever, to your heart's content. (There's lots more on X Windows in Chapter 7, "Looking Through X Windows.")

Trap **Any time you make changes to startup scripts, be sure you make a backup first.** It's possible—in fact, easy—to do something that'll prevent you from being able to log in. Your System Administrator will be fairly forgiving the first time, but successively less so after that. So always back up originals of your scripts to a safe place before you start messing with them.

Tip **Use rlogin to test your changes before you log all the way out.** This little trick can save you all sorts of embarrassment, besides reducing the cost and frequency of the required offerings on the altar of the systems gods. Whenever you make changes to any of your startup files, try the following before you go any further:

```
rlogin localhost
```

where *localhost* is replaced by the hostname of the machine you're currently on. The worst that can happen is you'll find out that what you just tried to do didn't work, and you can kill the **rlogin** and restore the saved version of the file.

Most of the examples in this chapter are done with the Korn shell, but with modest changes in syntax, they can be done with the C shell also.

The Korn shell uses two basic scripts to control its startup. The first, **.profile**, is processed only by the original login shell and resides in your home directory. This is the place to put terminal setting commands and environmental variables. However, once this script is read the first time, it's not normally read again for that session, unless we explicitly call it or in some other way force it to be read.

Tip **Put the things that can be exported into ~/.profile and have a second startup script.** This is so that if you want to spawn off another, secondary shell to do some work, you can do so without losing the primary one. This secondary shell, which might well be in a separate window if you're running X Windows, will only get the information from the login shell if that information is exported. And not everything can be exported. So, it makes sense to put the things that *can* be exported into ~/.**profile** and have a second startup script that is read by every Korn shell you may spawn. The usual name for this second startup script is **.kshrc**, and it should also reside in your home directory. After you create the file, nothing will happen until you take one additional step. You need to create a variable, **ENV**, and set it equal to the file you want to call then export the variable. This requires a pair of lines in your **.profile** file:

```
ENV=$HOME/.kshrc
export ENV
```

Just a quick note here. We used **~/.profile** in the preceding paragraph, and then used **$HOME/.kshrc** in the little extract that goes in your **.profile**. But there is, in fact, absolutely no difference when running Korn shell between **~** and **$HOME** when used this way. They both refer to your home directory, the place where you start out when you first log in to the system. We'll use them interchangeably, and you'll see both in other books.

Trap **If you're writing a shell script that must be interpreted by the Bourne shell, use the $HOME construct, since the Bourne shell doesn't support the ~ version.** In fact, it's probably a good idea to get in the habit of using **$HOME** in scripts as a matter of course. And it's easy enough to make that a **vi map!** command so you don't have to type it all out.

Tip **Use different .kshrc files for different projects.** We use this trick all the time. Instead of having **ENV** always refer to your home directory, have it point to the current directory first, and then, if it doesn't find a **.kshrc**, have it look at your home directory. This way, you can easily load a set of special aliases for each project and still have a default set for general use. Your initial login window, of course, will always see your default resource file, **$HOME/.kshrc**, since that will be the current directory when you log in. Figure 4-1 shows how to do it.

```
if [[ -f ./.kshrc ]]
then ENV='./.kshrc'
else ENV='$HOME/.kshrc'
fi
export ENV
```

Figure 4-1: *Using ENV to find a local resource file instead of the default.*

If you have a terminal with multiple windows available, or are running X Windows and have multiple windows open, then each window you open will look in the directory that's current at the time you open the window to see if there is a **.kshrc** present. If there is, it'll load that **.kshrc**. Unfortunately, however, it *won't* load your general one if there isn't a **.kshrc** in your current directory.

Trap **When running X Windows, your first window into a directory should be a login shell.** Add a -ls to the command line you use to call your X terminal for the initial window in a project directory. For example, this login shell will look to see if the current directory has a resource file. If it doesn't, then it will load your default resource file—**$HOME/ .kshrc**—and all subsequent windows loaded from that window will load the default resource file, too.

Tip **C shell users should use .cshrc to add customiza-
tions.** This file performs the same functions for **csh** users that
.kshrc does for Korn shell users. In the C shell, the login script
is the ~/.login, which equates to the Korn shell users'
~/.profile. However, the C shell also lets its users set default
actions when they log out. These are stored in the ~/.logout
script.

Get Rid of That Boring Old $ Prompt!

The Korn shell defines a variable, PS1, which is the normal prompt. So, if you
change the value of PS1, you change your prompt. This prompt can include the
values of other variables or any text string. For example, if you like to think of
yourself as the master of the computer, you might try this for a prompt:

```
PS1='How may I serve you, Master? '
```

Go ahead, try a few things. You can have some fun with this. But when you
get done fooling around, you'll probably want something more useful, so keep
reading.

Tip **Use the $PWD variable that is built into the Korn
shell to track your current directory.** Most of us are familiar
with the DOS prompt that tracks our current directory—
"PROMPT 4PSG". So, if you try to achieve the same thing in
UNIX, you might try this:

```
PS1="$PWD \$ "
```

Looks good at first glance. If you are in your home directory, it might look something like this:

```
/users/harold $
```

But what happens when you change to harold's bin directory? You type in this:

```
/users/harold $ cd bin
```

then ask for the identity of the present working directory,

```
/users/harold $ pwd
```

and end up with the following:

```
/users/harold/bin
/users/harold $
```

Maybe this isn't quite what you had in mind. That's because the double quotes allow the Korn shell to "see" the $PWD variable and interpret it. Once that happens, it's converted into a string and becomes static.

So, to prevent this, we enclose it in single quotes, which will stop the initial evaluation of the $PWD variable and allow it to be passed to the command line, where it will then get interpreted. So, now we type this:

```
$ PS1='$PWD \$ '
```

And when you change to harold's bin directory and ask for the present working directory, the prompt will show this:

```
/users/harold/bin $
```

Now the prompt will track the current directory as intended. The deep directory structures possible in UNIX can make for a pretty long prompt, however. For this reason, we like to use the following: a two line prompt with the current directory on the first line and the "$" on the second line. Type in this:

```
/users/harold $ PS1='$PWD ^J\$ '
```

to get a prompt that looks like this:

```
/users/harold
$
```

Now we have a nice two-line prompt that shows us the current directory.

Tip **Include your "pseudo terminal" in your prompt.** If you work on a machine that supports multiple pseudo terminals, keep track of which window you're working in by using this prompt:

```
PS1="\[$(tty|cut -c9-11)\]"'$PWD_$ '
```

The result will show this:

```
[p01]
```

followed by your directory name information.

Tip **Include the hostname in your prompt, so you know where you are.** If you work in a distributed environment, where you regularly log in to different machines from your "normal" machine, it can be a pain to keep track of which machine you're on. So include it in your prompt!

```
PS1="$(hostname)":'$PWD ^J \$ '
```

But when we do that on our system, we get this:

```
rci1.rci.com:/users/charlie
$
```

So, use the %% trick to strip off the unwanted stuff from the right side of the hostname. If you're stripping something off the left side, you use ## instead.

```
host='hostname'
PS1=${host%%.*}:'$PWD ^J \$ '
```

This puts the local hostname into the prompt, stripping out the domain name stuff that may be returned by running the **hostname** program.

Singles, Doubles & Gravès

Throughout this book, and other UNIX books, you will see three different kinds of quotation marks: single quotes ('), double quotes ("), and gravè quotes (`). Which is which and why should you care?

Each kind has a very different meaning to the shell. The single quote says to the shell, "Look, everything inside here is a plain, unadulterated string. Don't even *try* to check to see if you can interpret any of it. Just leave it alone and pass it on to the next process." Which means this is almost always the kind of quote you should use for an alias, because you want the first pass to simply ignore the inside of the quotes, and let it pass the contents to the second pass, which will then have the quotes stripped off and will be able to actually interpret what you are trying to do. But if you do have variables inside the single quotes, they won't be expanded but simply passed on, complete with their dollar signs.

Double quotes, on the other hand, are still enclosing strings. But now the shell is allowed to look inside to see if there are any special characters it should interpret. This allows it to expand any variable that it finds, for example, so that "$PWD" gets expanded immediately to the full current working directory. However, once the shell has expanded the inside of the double-quoted section, it passes the result to whatever follows as a literal, quoted string. This means that the inside of the double quotes will be evaluated when it is first seen and not again; so you can't use it in things like prompts and aliases where you want a secondary evaluation.

Finally, the gravè quotes—the ones that look like this: `—are very special, since they tell the shell to actually *run* the program inside the gravè quotes and replace the quoted section with the result of the quote. This means that `hostname` will be replaced in the command with the result of running the hostname program, which would be something like **rci1.rci.com** on our machine. Again, however, this is evaluated immediately, which means that the result is static. Many modern versions of the Korn shell have replaced this usage with a completely different-looking but essentially similar working construct - **$(hostname)**.

Tip **PATH too long for a prompt? Strip off the extra.** Use the # pattern-matching operator to strip out your home directory as shown in Figure 4-2.

```
$ pwd
$ /users/charlie
PS1='${PWD#$HOME*/}\$ '
/users/charlie $ cd /users/charlie/bin
bin $ cd
/users/charlie $ cd /bin
/bin $
```

Figure 4-2: *Take these steps to remove the home directory from your prompt when you're below the home directory (and only when you're below it).*

This prompt tracks directories under your home directory nicely; but when you're in your home directory you see the full current directory as part of your prompt. And whenever you wander out into the general part of the file system, you see where you are. Use ## in place of #$HOME in Figure 4-2, to see only the lowest directory in your prompt.

C Shell Users, Don't Despair

All this prompt stuff is nice if you are a Korn shell user, but what about the C shell users, you ask? Well, the good news is that these same tricks work pretty much in the same way for C shell users. The syntax is a bit different, of course, but the overall effect is pretty much the same. For example, suppose you want your basic prompt with the current directory in it:

```
set prompt="${cwd}% "
```

This should work on most systems where C shell supports the variable **cwd**. How about some of the other stuff? Well, you can easily set an alias, just like with the Korn shell. Here's our alias to get a long listing of the files that are in the current directory:

```
alias ll ls -lAF
```

Trap **Be careful where you put your aliases.** For startup files, the C shell uses **$HOME/.login** and **$HOME/.cshrc**. The **.login** is only read by the initial login shell, while the **.cshrc** file is read by all shells. So put your aliases in the **.cshrc** just as you would put them in the **.kshrc** file with the Korn shell.

Setting & Using Variables

You can make navigating in UNIX much easier by the use of variables. You should try to keep the use of aliases to a minimum, since every time you start a subshell, they must be evaluated; so reduce the number of aliases you need by creating variables and exporting them.

Working Directories Make Useful Variables

It's a nuisance to remember long path names to your frequently used directories. And if your needs or directories change, your scripts will break if they have the directories hard-coded. So, use a variable to describe the directory; then when your needs change, you get assigned to a new project or whatever, you only need to change your variables, and all your scripts and aliases will follow along.

For example, suppose you are working on a project with a group of coworkers. The files for the directory are stored in **/users/projects/newmodel/network**. Well you're not going to want to type that too often. So, create a variable that points to that directory—we'll call it PROJHOME—and include this in your **.profile**:

```
PROJHOME=/users/projects/newmodel/network
export PROJHOME
```

Now, you can change to the proper directory with

```
cd $PROJHOME
```

Tip **Add a variable to keep out prying eyes.** Let's say we have a special group working on this project, and, because it's super-secret, we don't want anyone else looking at our plans. So let's add another variable, PROJGRP, that we can use:

```
PROJGRP=netwrk
export PROJGRP
```

Now, a simple shell script will get us where we want to be, change to the necessary group, and fire off a copy of

WordPerfect to edit the functional specification for the project. The script is shown in Figure 4-3, where we've also defined the variable FSPEC to point to that functional spec.

```
# Shell Script to edit the functional spec
# for the current project
# Script stays the same as the projects change.
sg -a $PROJGRP
cd $PROJHOME
/usr/wp/xwp $FSPEC
```

Figure 4-3: *A script to keep everything private.*

Now, our shell script, which we called **proj** will automatically handle the whole process of getting us to where we want to be, firing off WordPerfect, and loading the working file. Sure beats doing all that by hand, doesn't it?

Terminal Tricks

For those of you stuck at a boring text terminal, here are a couple of little tricks you can try. If your terminal supports color but you still have this plain white text on a black background, use this:

```
alias -x blue='^[[37\;44m'
alias -x black='^[[37\;40m'
alias -x revrs='^[[7m'
alias -x norm='^[[0m'
```

The ^[in the above aliases is the escape character. You can enter this by pressing Ctrl-V, then Escape. Now, if you want a little blue screen with white text, just type **echo blue**. You could have included the **echo** as part of the alias, of course, but this would make the alias less useful. By doing it this way, with the **-x** parameter to alias, the "blue" is available from within your scripts. This is especially useful for using the **revrs** and norm aliases for highlighting text.

The following table shows the colors and their corresponding numbers for sprucing up your terminal's looks.

ANSI Escape Sequences for Changing Colors		
Position	Value	Color
overall	0	All attributes off
	1	bold
	4	underscore
	5	blink
	7	reverse video
	8	concealed
foreground	30	black
	31	red
	32	green
	33	yellow
	34	blue
	35	magenta
	36	cyan
	37	white
background	40	black
	41	red
	42	green
	43	yellow
	44	blue
	45	magenta
	46	cyan
	47	white

Values must be preceded by ^[[(Escape[) and be separated by an "escaped" semicolon (\;), and the sequence is terminated by an **m.**

Single-use variables don't need to be exported.
Reduce clutter in your environment. If you're going to use a variable only as a "local variable" inside a script, don't bother to export it in the script—and especially not in your dot-profile. Just create it in the script and use it there. When the script terminates, the variable will be unset once again.

Don't forget to export variables that you expect to use repeatedly. Put them in your **.profile** file (**.login** for the C shell) and they will be available throughout the entire session and in all your subshells, scripts or whatever. But don't forget to add a line that reads **export variable**.

You don't need to worry about removing variables.
They generally won't hurt anything. But if you are incurably fussy about such things, go ahead, knock yourself out! The command to remove a variable is:

```
unset variable.
```

To see the value of a variable, use the print command. You can see what a variable is set to by using **print "$variable"**. The **echo** command will also work for this, but it's better to use **print** since **echo** may behave differently on different systems. Also notice that we enclosed the variable name in double quotes. The shell will still see the $ inside the double quotes and expand the variable to its value.

DOS Commands in UNIX

Those of us who must constantly switch back and forth between UNIX and DOS machines are always having problems
with the differences. The commands in the two operating
systems are enough alike that our fingers are constantly con-
fused. The answer is to create a set of UNIX commands that
work like their DOS equivalents, and then do the same in
DOS. Here's a set of useful aliases. You'll probably find other
situations where you want to use an alias. Just add any other
alias names to the list, and then put them in your **.kshrc** file.

```
# DOS aliases, only available from an
# interactive shell so we don't slow down
# scripts.
case $- in
  *i*)
  # If $- matches *i*, this is a
  # shell, not a script
  alias copy='cp'
  alias move='mv'
  alias ren='mv'
  alias rd='rmdir'
  alias deltree='rm -r'
  alias cls='clear'
  alias dir='ls -l'
  alias type='cat' ;;
esac
```

We have a similar set we use from within DOS to handle
the problem. Create a file called **unix.bat** and stick it somewhere in your DOS path. Then, call the file from within your
autoexec.bat file. Here's our set of UNIX in DOS commands.

```
REM Only need to load DOSKEY inside here if
REM you aren't using it already. To load
REM it from within here, unREM the next
REM line. Note the fairly large buffer size.
REM You may need it.
REM doskey /bufsize=2048
doskey mv=move $*
doskey cp=copy $*
doskey ll=dir $* /p
doskey pwd=cd
doskey more=type $1 $b more
doskey cat=type $*
doskey man=help $1
doskey rm=del $*
doskey env=set | more
doskey grep=find $*
```

Finally, you may find that the single most annoying difference between the two environments is the difference between the UNIX text editor and the DOS text editor.

Tip **If you have to do much work in DOS, you'll miss your vi.** There are good replacements that run in the DOS world, however. One is Oak Hill Vi, from Oak Hill Software, Inc. in Scottsdale, AZ. The MKS Toolkit has an excellent **vi** as well as a complete replacement for DOS's **COMMAND.COM** shell that looks very much like UNIX.

Shell Script Shortcuts

The more you use UNIX, the more you'll find yourself writing shell scripts. Most will be short little things that serve a simple purpose. Some may be long, complicated scripts that have all sorts of error-checking in them. But whatever scripts you write, there are certain things they *should* have in common. Probably the easiest to forget, but the most important, is to always document your scripts. Yeah, right. Everyone always says that. But we really mean it. In fact, let's repeat it for emphasis.

Trap **Always document your shell scripts.** No matter how simple they are, it costs almost nothing to include a little header in them that gives key information—like the name of the file, the date it was created and the task it was supposed to perform. Sure, you know what it does. But you won't remember two weeks from now, much less two years from now.

Tip **Make a standard header file for every script.** Every script should have a header that you automatically include in each and every shell script that will be around long enough to get out of your ~/**tmp** directory. You can include what you want in yours, but we recommend that you add comments throughout the script as well. You'll thank yourself later.

Unique File Names

Let the system create unique file names for you. If you run a script every day like a backup of a set of important files onto a different file system, let UNIX do some of the work for you. If you need a file name generated every day, for example, let the date command do it. For example, Figure 4-4 shows a script that runs every day to make an export of a critical database. We use the **date** command to generate a file name. This makes it easy to keep track of which file is the most current, and at the same time lets us take this entire command and stick it into a crontab to make it happen automatically. For more on crontabs and running jobs automatically at specified times, see Chapter 6, "Running Programs."

```
#======================================================================
#
#              Filename: db_exp.ksh
#
#               Author: Sharon Crawford
#
#         Description: Script to create an automatic export of the database.
#
#    Last Modification: 12/24/94-Modified to compress file on creation - cpr
#            Prev. Mod: Added absolute path to exp - 10/23/93 - cpr
#
#======================================================================
#
# Setup Oracle Environment
#
./scripts/oracle_setup DUMMY
#
# Run Script
#
print \n
print 'Executing script  db_exp.ksh'
ORACLE_SID=rci; export ORACLE_SID
file=/safety/`date +%b%d`.dmp  # Create unique filename with today's date
#
#  Put Command into variable -
oracmd="/oracle/bin/exp system/rcipw file=$file grants=y indexes=y full=y"
#
print "Executing command ...
print \"$oracmd \"
$oracmd
# Execute the compression on the created file to reduce space
# This could be simply piped from the export, but is separate for
# historical reasons.
compress $file
exit
```

Figure 4-4: *A well-documented script.*

Tip

If you only need a file as a temporary storage place, let the system do the work. Let UNIX worry about cleaning up after you and keeping track of the file name. Some commands need a file as an intermediate storage spot, so use UNIX's built in functions to create and delete the temporary file name. The **mktemp** command exists in many implementations of UNIX, but if it doesn't exist in yours, you can let the shell generate a name. If **mktemp** exists, try this:

```
filename='mktemp'
```

Then, when the script is finished, just add a final line to clean up after yourself:

```
rm $filename
```

If your version of UNIX doesn't support **mktemp**, use the built-in functionality of the shell to do the work:

```
filename="/tmp/$LOGNAME.$SECONDS"
```

This will generate a file name based on your login name, and the number of seconds since you started this shell. Just remember to remove the file when you are done with it. Otherwise your System Administrator is likely to become grumpy about cleaning up after you.

Moving On

In this chapter, you've seen some of the ways you can customize your environment to make life easier for yourself. We'll see even more ways when we take a look at X-Windows in Chapter 7, "Looking Through X Windows." But first we'll explore printing. We'll see how to send jobs to the printer, control the options for the printer, and how to cancel a print job that went wrong, along with some tips on keeping everyone happy in a shared printing environment.

Printing Magic

When you work with computers, sooner or later you'll need to print your work onto paper. Computers were supposed to usher in the era of the "paperless office," but realizing that ideal seems to be far in the future.

In the meantime, even more paper is being generated because printing a copy of this or that is so much easier now than it was B.C. (Before Computers). In this chapter, we will explore some of the ways you can make your printing tasks easier and more effective, and also give you some tips for avoiding as well as fixing trouble when it arises.

Because UNIX was designed to be a multiuser, multitasking environment, the early designers realized that they needed to allow people to continue working on the system while printing was going on. Printing is a slow process, even on the fastest printers, and it doesn't require much raw processing power. To make everyone wait while the printer was doing its thing would be a serious waste of time and resources.

So UNIX borrowed from the mainframe world: it sends all printing tasks or "jobs" to a spooler. The printing spooler is a background task (known as a *daemon*) that's always there waiting for something to do. When you send a job to the printer, you're actually sending it to the printer daemon, which first stores it on the hard disk in a temporary file then sends it to the printer a piece at a time. This way, you (and the rest of the users on the system) can go on about business. Since the spooler needs only a tiny portion of the available processor time to get its job done, it prints your job without tying up the main processor.

If everything goes well, you click on the Print button in WordPerfect, select the printer you want your updated résumé to go to, and send it off. By the time you walk over to the printer, the job is coming out, and you grab it before anyone else has a chance to see it. No problem.

But wait. Someone else has started a print job on that printer that will take an hour to complete, and your résumé is stuck behind that print job! Hmmm. Think your boss will mind if you just sort of hang around the printer? It's time to figure out how to handle this, and lots of other little problems that crop up in a shared printing environment.

Printing Now—the "Normal" Way

Most printing you do will be like this: you finish editing a document, and you want to print it. If you are working inside an application program, such as WordPerfect or IslandCalc or whatever, you just follow the print commands appropriate to that program, select the destination you want, and go pick up the output when it is done.

But much of what you want to print may well not be from inside an application. It may be text you have created using UNIX's native tools, or it may be just files you need to print.

On System V UNIX systems, this standard printing command will be

```
lp notes
```

If you're on a Berkeley UNIX system, the standard command to print a file is

```
lpr notes
```

We'll be showing the System V version of the commands first, and the Berkeley system version second. You'll see that they're very similar.

Tip **Use the LPDEST environment variable to change the default printer destination.** Your System Administrator (or on some systems the LP Administrator) can set an overall default printer for each machine on the network. But if you usually want your output to go to a different printer, add the different destination to your **.profile** file:

```
LPDEST=laser ; export LPDEST
```

This will set your default printer to "laser" instead of whatever the particular default for the machine may be. It can be useful for using different printers for different projects as well.

In Berkeley systems, you usually substitute **PRINTER** for the **LPDEST** instruction shown above.

Tip **Use the -ddest option to override the default destination.** You can easily override your default destination for any particular print job by adding a destination to the **lp** command. If you knew you had a memo that you wanted to print on the laser printer next to the department secretary's desk, for example, you could use this command:

```
lp -dsec_laser mymemo
```

Berkeley systems use the **-P***dest* option to accomplish the same thing.

The nobanner Option

Tired of wasted paper and that silly banner page? Use the nobanner option to get rid of it. This isn't such a hot idea, by the way, if you work with a shared printer on a network that gets a lot of different print requests, because there'll be no way to know whose print job just came out of the printer. But on small networks or where the printer is physically close to you, by all means dump that banner.

```
lp -onobanner notes
```

Other systems have other shortcuts for this—usually **-onb** or **-ob** but the long form is usually the same on all systems. For Berkeley systems, the option is **-h** for no header.

Tip **Use the -n option to control the number of copies that will print.** When you need more than one copy, just put the number on the command line:

```
lp -n 3 notes
```

The above command will give you three copies of the notes. Berkeley uses **#***n* where *n* is the number you want.

Tip **Tired of hanging around the printer, waiting for your job?** Let the print spooler send you a message when the job is finished. Use the following command:

```
lp -m notes
```

The print spooler will send you a mail message when it finishes. If you use **-w**, it will write the message directly to your terminal when the job finishes. Use this option with caution—lots of programs don't like having messages dumped to the terminal while they're running. If you aren't logged in when the job finishes, the message is mailed instead.

For Berkeley users, the mail option is the same —**-m**.

Tip **Control the way your printed job looks using printer-specific options.** Each printer type or model will have a list of possible options that it will support. These range from the fairly simple ones available for dot matrix printers to the more complicated ones for a typical laser printer. You can add as many options as you want to the command line, but remember that each option requires a separate **-o** *option*.

The printing on a UNIX system is controlled by a script that knows which options the particular printer will support and which escape sequence is required to set each option. This script file, which can be modified by the System Administrator to add special characteristics for an individual printer, usually resides in the **/usr/spool/lp/model** directory.

To see what options are supported for your printer, you can print this file out. But, in general, these include options to control the character spacing and font type, as well as the quality and orientation of the printout. On typical dot matrix printers, for example, the options may include such things as using elite or compressed type and whether to print in draft mode or near letter quality.

On a typical laser printer, options likely will include the ability to change fonts, and even optional settings for different font cartridges or paper trays. The quality of the printer support will depend on a variety of factors, including how recent the UNIX version is.

Printing Later—Delayed Magic

One of the problems with working in a shared printer environment is that you can't always use the printer as you want to because it might disrupt others on the system. An example of this is large print jobs that could tie the printer up for long periods. How long is a long period? This depends on your environment.

Trap If you share a printer with a small group—three or four other people—and you ask permission first, you can probably get away with a print job that takes a half-hour or even an hour without causing trouble.** But try that on a centralized printer shared by 25 or 30 users and listen to the screams.

There are a couple of ways to handle the shared-printer problem, depending on how your system is set up. Probably the simplest one is to fire off the print job on your way out the door at night. If that's not an option, here are some ideas to keep the peace, at least where printing's concerned.

Tip Use the hold option to get your file ready for printing but don't actually start it till later.** If you use the hold option when printing that big job, it'll be held until you tell it to actually go to the printer. Meanwhile, however, it's been fed to the spooler and is ready and waiting. Then when the printer will be free for an extended period, you can start it up. To print the file **bigdocument** to the printer **netlaser** but hold it until you say go, try this:

```
lp -dnetlaser -H hold -m bigdocument
```

Then, when you want to start the printing, enter this:

```
lp -i requestid -H resume
```

This still requires some degree of planning and attention on your part, but at least you know everything's ready and waiting. There's a second problem with it as well: you need to know what the request id is for the job you want to resume. As you can see in Figure 5-1, you'll be told the request id when you first issue the print command, so you should write it down and hope that when it's time to resume the job you'll be able to remember where you wrote it.

```
$ lp -dlaser -H hold /tmp/hugefile
request id is laser-7566 (1 file)
$ lpstat -u
laser-7566      sharon        5425111   May 20 16:20 being held
cprdot-7570     root             7126   May 20 16:21
cprdot-7571     stanley         23450   May 21 16:21
$ lp -i laser-7566 -H resume
$
```

Figure 5-1: The **lp** command will tell you the request id for your print job.

Tip **Use lpstat to find out the status of your print jobs.**
This command gives you all sorts of information, but in its simplest form it tells you what jobs you have in what queue. Or to see what is in all the printer queues, use the **-u** option.

```
lpstat -u
```

Without the **-u** option, all you will see are the jobs that belong to you.

Tip

Use the at command to schedule a print job for later.
If your System Administrator has given you permission, you can use the **at** command to schedule a print job for later execution. We'll look at the **at** command in more detail in Chapter 6, "Running Programs," but for the moment here's a simple example to run a series of print commands at 5:30 pm.

```
at 05:30pm < commandfile
```

where *commandfile* is a file you have created that contains each of the commands you want executed at 5:30, one line to a command, like this:

```
lp -dlaser -o 12 bigdoc.txt
lp -ddotmatrix -o draft -o condensed→
  biggerdoc.txt
lp -dsec_laser -o landscape notice.post
```

Formatting for Fun & Profit

Okay, so maybe the header is a bit of a come-on. But you should be able to have some fun and at least save both time and money, which is a form of profit, after all.

If you want your print jobs from UNIX to be something other than plain old dull Courier, then you're going to have to take some steps to make that happen. You *could* go out and buy a high-priced word processor or an even higher-priced desktop publishing package (and there certainly are some excellent ones that run on most UNIX platforms).

If you intend to do a lot of heavy-duty formatting and want to see what your document looks like before you actually print it, then you're probably going to need one of these programs. But if all you need to do is spiff up your output a bit or include an equation or graphic, you probably don't really need to use anything but the tools you already have on your system. And if you are comfortable with simply entering the commands to print double-spaced in bold, and you have faith that that will happen without your actually being able to see the result until you print it, then you can publish whole books with the native UNIX tools.

The pr Command

The built-in **pr** utility handles all sorts of simple little formatting chores with ease. It can handle multicolumn output, set tab stops, double-space a file, add a left margin, expand tabs to spaces, convert spaces back to tabs or add line numbers to a file. We're not talking desktop publishing here, but for simple tasks it's quick and easy.

Tip **Use the -d option to pr to double-space your file.** UNIX editors like **vi** don't want to give you double-spaced text, so to get it, you need to run the job through **pr** as you print it:

```
pr -d filename | lp -
```

This takes the input file and double-spaces it, sending the result straight to the default printer and leaving the original unchanged. This will also add a header that includes the date and time as well as the page and file name.

Tip **Use the -on option to add a left margin.** Again, **vi** isn't going to give you a left margin, and it can be awkward to add it manually, so just run the file through **pr** to handle this little task:

```
pr -d -o10 | lp -
```

Now the document is double-spaced and has a left margin of 10 characters added.

Figures 5-2 and 5-3 show the file before and after the above command line.

```
Perhaps you have some extremely important text that
you need to print. Perhaps the words are so
brilliant that you're sure they don't
need even a smidgin of editing, but editors, being
the quixotic creatures they are, insist on
```

Figure 5-2: *A simple little document before **pr** has done its job.*

```
      Perhaps you have some extremely important text that

      you need to print. Perhaps the words are so

      brilliant that you're sure they don't

      need even a smidgin of editing, but editors, being

      the quixotic creatures they are, insist on
```

Figure 5-3: *The same document with a left margin double-spaced.*

Remove hard tabs and realign your tab stops with the -eck option. One very annoying trait of **vi** is that it uses "hard" tabs. You can change the amount of space each one represents with **:set ts=***n* where *n* is the spacing. But when you go to print the document or view it without setting **ts** the same, everything gets jumbled up, as shown in Figure 5-4.

```
This is      a     test of   the   tab  character  at     3.

Column1            Column2         Column3
First                    Second          Third
a                        b                      c
123                23456                789
```

Figure 5-4: *The hard tabs result when using* **vi**.

Well, here's a simple little shell script to convert tabs to spaces, lined up with the tab stops every three spaces. You could spruce this one up to have a variable number of spaces for your tab stops, add error checking, whatever. It works and it's simple.

```
# File ~/bin/detab — removes tabs from a
#   file and converts to spaces
# File name remains the same.
pr -t -e3 $1 > /tmp/tabtmp
cp /tmp/tabtmp $1
```

This little gem is something we added to our *~/.exrc* file as a **map** so we can run it from within **vi**. We have it mapped to Ctrl-T for tabs:

```
map ^T ^[1G!G pr -te3^M
```

Voila! Just hit Ctrl-T, and all your tabs are converted to spaces, and your columns still line up nice and neat, with three-space indents as shown in Figure 5-5.

```
This is    a    test of   the   tab  character  at    3.

Column1    Column2    Column3
First      Second     Third
a          b          c
123        23456      789
```

Figure 5-5: *The proper way to line things up.*

Tip 77 **Need to put the tabs back? Use the -in option to replace spaces with tabs.** If you need to make sure you have tab characters in a file you put spaces into, use the **pr** command again, but this time use **-i** to insert tab characters. This is useful if, for example, you'll later be importing the text into a word processing program that uses a variable-spaced font, one that will correctly interpret the tab character.

Tip 77 **Turn a list into a multicolumn format.** Here, a simple **-n** will tell **pr** to convert your list of names into an *n* column list. If you want columns ordered across instead of down the page, add a **-a** to the command.

```
pr -3a -t names > names.out
```

This will convert the list of names into a three-column list. Combine this with UNIX's built-in sorter to get a sorted list in three-column format.

```
sort names | pr -3a -t > sorted.names
```

The before and after appear in Figures 5-6 and 5-7.

```
Alan
Armando
Barbara
Cindy
Dave
Esther
Frank
Janna
Olivia
Perla
```

Figure 5-6: *Our unsorted list of names.*

```
Alan        Armando       Barbara
Cindy       Dave          Esther
Frank       Janna         Olivia
Perla
```

Figure 5-7: *The list sorted into easy-to-read format.*

Stop the Presses!

Aaack! You just inadvertently sent your 200-page print job to the printer, only to realize that you made a crucial mistake, right in the middle of it. What to do? Let it run to the end and throw the entire thing out and reprint it? Seems an awful waste of paper, trees and time, doesn't it? So, use the **cancel** command to cancel the print job you just sent. This is the form for the cancel command:

```
cancel [request-id] [printer]
```

which means that you can either cancel a job by specifying the request id or by specifying the printer and thereby cancelling the job on that printer.

Trap **You can only cancel a print job that you created.** To cancel someone else's print job requires (ta-da!) the Superuser's permission.

Tip **Use the lpstat command to get the current status of your print request.** Use this command, along with the **-u** *yourname* to get a list of just your current print jobs. Jobs that are currently printing will show as **on** *printer*, where *printer* is the name of the printer. Figure 5-8 shows that "sharon" has two jobs queued up for the laser printer, and the first one has already started printing.

```
laser-7586     sharon     12345    May 23 13:53 on laser

laser-7586     sharon     7654     May 23 13:54
```

Figure 5-8: *The report back from the **lpstat** command.*

Tip **Use lpstat to find where your job is printing.** In an environment where you may have several essentially similar printers, often you will specify that your print job should go to a *class* of printers, rather than a particular printer. In this case, use the **lpstat** command with the **-o -l** options to see not only which jobs you have queued but which printers they are queued for. Where you have used a printer class instead of a specific printer as the destination, you will see something like Figure 5-9:

```
laser-7586          sharon          7654      May 23 13:54
       on laser
dotmatrix-7896 sharon              89987      May 23 14:04
       assigned fastdot
```

Figure 5-9: *A more detailed report from **lpstat**.*

Here, you have one job currently printing on printer *laser* while a second job is assigned to *fastdot* but hasn't started printing yet.

Moving On

In this chapter, we've covered some ways to convert your files on the computer into printed form. We've printed now or delayed the job until later, and we've even done some reformatting of the document. In the next chapter, we get away from UNIX in its ugliest duckling manifestation. We look at the X Window System, in which UNIX becomes a swan and you're forever cured of Microsoft Windows envy.

Running Programs

Well, getting the look and feel you want, using an editor, finding out where files are located and how to print them—all this stuff is nice. But after all, the real reason you are using this thing is to get some *work* done, right? And if you want to get some work done, or your boss seems to have this weird fixation on actually seeing some results, chances are you'll have to launch at least one program occasionally.

Starting a Single Program

Actually, UNIX is always running several programs all the time, so you can't ever just run a single program. But most of that happens in the background and behind the scenes (like all magic), so we'll just let it stay there for the moment. You'll remember from Chapter 2 that each file on your machine has a set of separate permissions. These include permission to read the file, write to the file and execute the file. By execute we mean make the file *run*—as in actually *do* something.

It's important to understand that very few programs, and probably none you will have to worry about (unless you end up as a Superuser) are actually executed directly by UNIX.

They are in fact executed by the shell. Whether you are running Bourne, Korn, C, or one of the less common shells, it's actually the shell that interprets what you type at the prompt, and it's the shell that issues the necessary commands to start up the program. It's also the responsibility of the shell to examine the permissions for the file and decide if you even have the right to run the program. So, if you don't first set the execute permission bit for your program, you aren't going to get very far with it.

Trap Use chmod +x to make your program executable.
This seems pretty obvious. But when you try to execute some nice little program you wrote to say "Hello, World!" (okay, we know that's hardly original, but sometimes one must bow to tradition), and you get something that looks like Figure 6-1, you'll know you forgot to give your file permission to execute.

```
~/bin:$ hello
ksh: hello: cannot execute
~/bin:$ chmod +x hello
~/bin:$ hello


        Hello, World!


~/bin:$
```

Figure 6-1: *This is what happens when you forget to make a program executable—and how to fix it.*

Tip **Create a simple shell script to automatically make your shell scripts executable.** This is sort of a recursive fix. Use a shell script to make your shell scripts execute. You can get fancy about this, if you really want, but we use just the simple little **vix** script shown in Figure 6-2.

```
#!/bin/ksh
#       Filename: vix
#       Desciption: simple shell script to create and edit
#                   a file and make it executable all in one pass.
# Last modified: 7/24/92 by slc
cd $HOME/bin              # Put all scripts in bin directory
vi $1
chmod +x $1
```

Figure 6-2: *Use a shell script to call your editor and change the permissions all in a single step.*

Tip **Control which shell your script is executed by, without having to change scripts.** Figure 6-2 showed a little trick we were going to save for Chapter 11, where we talk about shell script secrets, but since it's in this figure, we'll talk about it here. Notice the first line of the script, which reads

#!/bin/ksh

You would think that this is a comment, since it starts with the # character. But what it really does is tell whatever shell is executing the file to execute **/bin/ksh** (the Korn shell) and feed it the rest of the file. We'll use this trick later in Chapter 11 when programming with **perl** to actually have perl do the executing, instead of a shell.

Tip

Use the history list to re-issue commands. One of the most useful features the C shell added to UNIX was the ability to re-use a command rather than have to retype it. The Korn shell takes this even further. You can not only re-use your commands, but you can edit them with your favorite editor, right there on the command line. To simply re-use the most recent command that started with the letter v, for example, **r v** will recycle the last command you issued that begins with v. So if you are editing a file then executing it to see if you have it like you want it then going back in to try again, this trick makes it easy to cycle back and forth between the two commands. The more of the command you include, the more precise the match. For example, if your last four commands had been:

```
vi .kshrc
.  .kshrc
vi .exrc
vi notes
```

then **r v** would recall the **vi notes** command, while **r vi .** would recall the **vi .exrc** command, and **r vi .k** would recall the **vi .kshrc** command.

Tip

Use familiar editor commands to cycle through and edit your previous commands. If you're using the Korn shell and include the following in your profile, you can actually use **vi** to edit your commands right at the command line, cycling through them and then modifying them as needed.

```
EDITOR=vi ; export EDITOR
```

This, plus the presence of a ~/.sh_history file tells the Korn shell to use the familiar **vi** editor commands to let you edit your command lines before you issue them. Just press the Escape key to enter **vi** mode, and then use the cursor movement keys, "j", "k", "l" and "h" to move through the commands. Press the "k" to move up one line to the previous command, "j" to go down and so forth. Once you find the command you want, just hit the Enter key to re-issue it, or use the editor keys to modify it. This is harder to explain than it is to do. Just try it. This feature alone is enough reason to switch from the C shell to the Korn shell.

If You're a Confirmed Emacs User, Don't Despair

You don't have to know **vi** commands to use command-line editing in the Korn shell. Just add this line to your **.profile** file, and you can now use your **emacs** keys to move through your command history and edit the commands.

```
VISUAL=emacs ; export VISUAL
```

Why the difference between the environment variables we set for the two modes? Actually, either one will work. Some sources seem to prefer setting **EDITOR** while others seem to prefer setting **VISUAL**. But both appear to work the same. The one thing we wouldn't recommend, however, is setting them to different values. If you do, **VISUAL** will win.

Basic Plumbing—Piping & Redirection

If you're like most people, you hate and fear anything that looks like it might be plumbing. But in UNIX, you can actually do plumbing without getting wet (and if you make a mess, it's easier to clean up).

Redirection and piping in UNIX are analogous to plumbing, in that they're about controlling flow, making sure data goes where you want it to be. You can redirect the input, so that instead of coming from the keyboard it comes from a file. Or you can redirect the output so that instead of going to your monitor it goes into a file. And finally, you can take the output from one program and feed (pipe) it into another program.

Probably the first kind of redirection we all learn to do is output redirection. That means getting all the stuff we usually don't want to see off of the screen and into a file, where we can find it if we need it but otherwise not be bothered. To redirect the output from a program to a file, use the greater-than symbol ">". For example, to sort a file of names:

```
sort names > names.sorted
```

The second kind of redirection is input redirection. This uses the less-than symbol "<". With this, instead of a program getting its input from the keyboard, it gets it from a file. So, for example, to mail a file to Dale in Engineering that includes the text of a new proposal he needs, you'd use this command:

```
mail dale < proposal.txt
```

The third and most important kind of redirection is piping, which uses the bar or pipe symbol "|". A pipe takes the output of one program and feeds it to another program. So, for example, to take that really cool game you just got from your favorite ftp site on the Internet, expand it and un-tar it, all in one operation:

```
cat newgame.taz | zcat | tar xvf -
```

We'll talk more about tar format in Chapter 10.

Piping is central to the way much of UNIX works. Because it was originally designed to run on very small machines with limited memory, it's made up of literally hundreds of small programs. Each one does little by itself; but as a group of programs working together in the UNIX repertoire, each becomes part of a powerful command set.

Multitasking Magic

Unlike DOS, UNIX is by its very nature a multitasking operating system. So you can take advantage of that multitasking capability to run multiple programs or jobs. If you are running the X Windows System, this is as simple as opening up another window and starting up the second program. But even on a simple, character-based terminal you can take advantage of this in most implementations of UNIX. At the very least, you should be able to send a job to the background to let it run while you start something else.

Tip **Use the & following a program's command line to send it to the background.** Some jobs, like long **find** operations or program compilations usually tend to take a while to complete and normally don't require any input from you. Send these jobs into the background by putting an ampersand (&) after the command line. This gives you back your prompt, while the job you have *spawned* goes on about its business. Figure 6-3 shows a simple example that a System Administrator might run periodically to clean up some large files that were taking up disk space.

```
/# find / -name core -a -mtime +7 -exec rm -f {} \; &
[1]      8373
/# jobs
[1] + Running find / -name core -a -mtime +7 -exec rm -f {} \; &
/# jobs
[1] + Done     find / -name core -a -mtime +7 -exec rm -f {} \; &
/#
```

Figure 6-3: *Use the & operator to move big jobs into the background.*

Tip

Use the jobs command to check on your background jobs. As you can see in Figure 6-3, the **jobs** command will tell you what the status of your background job is. If the job has finished, you will see the job number and a "Done" after it. The other possibilities are "Running" and "Stopped." What about the "+" we see there? That indicates that this job was the most recently invoked job that's in the background. The next most recently invoked would be shown with a "-".

Tip

Use the fg command to bring a background job back into the foreground. This command will bring the most recently invoked job back into the foreground. If the job has been stopped (suspended) for some reason, it will restart when it comes into the foreground. If you have several jobs running in the background and you need to bring a job other than the most recent one to the foreground, use one of the ways listed in the table below to refer to the job. Thus, to bring the **grep** operation you started several jobs ago back to the foreground,

```
fg %grep
```

This will bring the **grep** job into the foreground. From there you can send it back into the background, suspend (stop) it, interrupt (kill) it or simply wait for it to finish.

Ways to Reference a Background Job

Reference	Background Job Referenced
1. %*n*	The job whose number is *n*
2. %*string*	The most recent job whose command line begins with *string*
3. %?*string*	The most recent job whose command line contains *string*
4. %+	The most recent job
5. %%	Another way to get at the most recent job
6. %-	The second most recent job

Tip

Use the bg command to send a job to the background. Suppose you started a search for the changes in your doctoral thesis and realize it's going to take a lot longer than you expected. Fortunately, you had it set for all the output of the **diff** command to go into a log file, so you can just suspend the job and send it into the background. The usual command to suspend a job is Ctrl-Z (unless you have changed it with **stty**). Press Ctrl-Z, then type **bg** to send the job into the background. Then restart. If you want to see how it's going, you can just **tail** the log file.

Trap

Don't send to background a job that needs input from you or one that will send lots of output to the screen. If a job is in the background and needs some input from you, it will just sit there waiting for you to respond. Not quite what you had in mind, one suspects. And if the job will produce a lot of messages that would go on your screen unless you had sent them to a log file, these messages will all end up on your screen, right in the middle of what you're trying to do. Again, probably an annoyance, to say the least.

The best way to handle these potential unwanted interruptions is to redirect the output to a log file, with any errors sent to a separate error file. Here's an example of how to do that:

```
diff thesis thesis.edited > /tmp/→
    edit.log 2> /tmp/edit.err &
```

Now the command will run in the background and not bother you with output you aren't ready to deal with anyway. The **2>** means to send standard error to where we have pointed to, in this case

```
/tmp/edit.err
```

Using Redirection

Use redirection to send both normal program output and error messages to a file. In fact, if you want to send them to the same file, you use a special combination. A typical example of this might be when you're running a backup or a long compilation. You aren't bothered with the output from it while you are doing other things, but when the compile or backup is done, you can quickly check to see where any problems were. Here, we use a special way of describing the pipe of standard error.

```
make > /tmp/make.log 2>&1 &
```

This uses redirection to send normal messages from our make to a log file, and any error messages will go to the same place. Here, **2>&1** means "take standard error and redirect it to standard output." But since we have already told standard output to go to a log file, both will go there.

Tip **Use the tee command to send output to both a log file and the screen.** This lets you start a process, like a backup, where you want to be able to see if anything untoward happens but store all the messages from the command in a log file as well. This is particularly useful on a windowed system where you can continue to work and yet keep your eye on what's happening.

```
make 2>&1 | tee /tmp/make.log &
```

Now when your **make** more or less barfs all over itself, you'll have the pleasure of watching all those lovely warning messages scroll by on the screen and know they're saved to a log file. Later you can stare solemnly at them and pretend you actually know what they mean before you go twiddle with the make file and try again.

Being a Nice User—Setting Priorities

When you work in a multitasking and multiuser environment, you can easily bring the entire system to a virtual halt by starting one or more jobs that are very demanding of memory and the processor. Even if you're the only person on the system, starting a big compile job in the background may slow your foreground task to a snail's pace. Naturally, UNIX has a solution. The **nice** command decreases the command's priority by increasing its *niceness*. Unfortunately, this particular command is different in virtually every version of UNIX and can even vary from shell to shell. But the general effect is the same; you can reduce the amount of CPU time a particular process requires by starting it with **nice**. So, for details of how your version is implemented, check the manual pages for "nice."

```
man nice
```

Note that you can make a command be nicer, but, unless you are the Superuser, you generally can't make a command have a higher priority than it normally would have (in other words, be *less* nice). Also, it doesn't generally make sense to reduce the priority of jobs that are essentially I/O bound, since these jobs don't require much of the processor's resources anyway.

Trap **Don't use nice on a foreground job.** If your system gets bogged down anyway and you have given your foreground job a "nice" command, you may not be able to get its attention long enough to suspend or kill it. You'll be essentially locked out until the job finishes.

Scheduling Incantations—Time-Related Commands

UNIX gives you the ability to schedule jobs to run at some specific time in the future, or even run automatically every day, every week, the first Sunday of every month or on almost any other regular schedule you choose. There are several ways to do this, depending on what you need.

Putting a Job to Sleep

The simplest of the time-related commands is the **sleep** command. This does just what it sounds like it would—it puts commands or script files to sleep for the number of seconds you specify. So, why would you want to do this? Well, it can be useful to display a message on the screen in the midst of a shell script, for example, leaving it there long enough for you to see it. A good example of this is when you are going to do something irrevocable, such as delete a file or a set of files, and you want to give yourself a chance to back out if things don't look right, but if you don't interrupt the process it will go through automatically. Here, what you do is **print** or **echo** the command that is about to be executed to the screen and then let the script sleep for five or ten seconds. If things don't look right, you can break out of the script and fix it before it's too late. Or, if you need to fire off several processes, each of which grabs lots of resources when it first starts but then settles down, you can use **sleep** in the script that starts them in order to space them out a bit.

Make Yourself an Alarm Clock

Use the **sleep** command as a simple alarm clock or reminder. This is another effective use of this command. There are more complicated ways to do this, but if you tend to get involved in what you're doing and lose track of the time, here's a simple way to remind yourself that you need to leave for a meeting in 15 minutes.

```
(sleep 900; print "Time for your meeting→
    with Lance!")&
```

This will go happily and quietly to sleep in the background, eating almost no resources, and in 15 minutes (900 seconds) will wake up and print out the message to the screen then terminate. The trick here is the use of the parentheses () around the command, which groups the entire command together into a subshell and allows you to send it together into the background.

Trap 🦎 **Use the sleep command to give yourself a chance to back out of a command.** We like to do this whenever we have either an irrevocable command or one that has automatically built a fairly complicated string that might have gotten munged in transit. Just add a **sleep 5** to the command to allow yourself time to interrupt the script before it actually executes. Figure 6-4 shows how this works:

```
Print "Removing all old files in directory $tmpdir using command
line..."
Print "\n\t find $tmpdir -atime +7 -exec rm {} \;\n"
Print "If this doesn't look right, press Ctrl-C to interrupt the
script"
Print "within the next 5 seconds."
sleep 5
find $tmpdir -atime +7 -exec rm {} \;
```

Figure 6-4: *Using the **sleep** command as a hedge against disaster.*

In this simple example, the variable **$tmpdir** will, of course, get expanded to whatever temporary directory you are clearing out. The result of the command will be to delete all the files in the temporary directory that have not been accessed in the past seven days.

The at Command

The **at** command lets you schedule an activity at a specific time in the future. Unlike **sleep**, you can enter a clock time, not just X minutes in the future.

Tip

Use the at command to schedule an event to occur at some time in the future. A good example of this is to schedule a big compile to occur when everyone's gone home for the night, so that the system won't get bogged down by it. The **at** command is pretty flexible about what it will accept for time descriptions, but a bit unusual otherwise. The best way to handle it is to list the commands to be executed in a simple file, and then redirect that file into the **at** command, along with the time it is to be executed. Understand that all commands executed by the **at** command will be executed using the Bourne shell, not the C or the Korn shell, so don't depend on any specific features of these more versatile shells. The **at** command will understand all of the following time parameters, as well as many others.

* at 10:15am - At 10:15 am, today (tomorrow, if it is already after 10:15am)

* at 1120pm Jun 17 - At 11:20 pm, on June 17th

* at 1 am Sunday - At 1:00 am next Sunday morning

* at 18:00 Monday next week - At 6 pm, next Monday

* at now +2 hours - Two hours from now

As you can see, this is pretty flexible. The syntax for running a backup routine of the /users file system to the DAT tape drive at 1:00 am tomorrow morning would be

```
at 0100 tomorrow < backup.users
```

where **backup.users** contained the single line:

```
tar -cvf /dev/dat /users > /tmp/
backup.users.log
```

which includes the **tar** command with the necessary options to write a new archive out to the DAT drive and keep a record of all the messages in a log file for later perusal.

The cron Command

If your System Administrator has given you permission to do so, you may create a **crontab** to automate your tasks. This is a file that describes one or more actions that you want to occur on a regular basis.

Tip **Create a crontab to automatically run programs repeatedly.** You can schedule jobs to run once a month, every night, every Friday or whatever. There are lots of possibilities. The **crontab** file consists of 6 fields:

* minute   A number from 0-59 indicating the minute the command will be run.

* hour   A number from 0-23 indicating the hour for the command to be run.

* day of month   A number from 1-31 indicating the day of the month to run the command.

* month   A number from 1-12 indicating the month to run the command.

* day of week   A number from 0-6 (Sunday to Saturday) for the command to be run.

* the command
    line to be run

If a field contains an asterisk (*), it means all possible values for that field. So, for example, to run a backup of your home directory every night to the floppy drive, you might have the following as a **crontab**:

```
15 1 * * * /usr/bin/tar uvf /dev/rfd0 $HOME
> /tmp/$LOGNAME.bak.log 2>&1
```

One thing to note about this command is that we were careful to direct the output from the command to a log file, and we also made sure that any error messages went there as well. Otherwise, the output from the command will be sent to the console, which could cause other problems. Also, like the **at** command, all **crontab** jobs are executed using the default Bourne shell. The location of your **crontab** file is in **/usr/spool/cron/crontabs/***username*. But you should first create the file in your home directory and then submit it to the **cron** process with

```
crontab cronfile
```

which will overwrite any existing **crontab** file with the new one.

Trap **Always make a copy of your old crontab file before you submit a new one.** We find it's distressingly easy to forget that any new **crontab** will overwrite your old one. So, we have a little script that first saves a copy of our existing **crontab** then submits the new one. This way, we automatically make a copy and submit the new one. The relevant lines from the script are

```
cd $HOME
crontab -l > oldcron.$(date +%m%d%H%M)
crontab new.cron
```

This saves a copy of the old **crontab** in a time and datestamped file, and then submits the new cronfile, which we always keep in "new.cron." This makes it easy to keep a copy of your old **crontab** files.

Tip **Use crontab -l to see your current automatically scheduled jobs.** The -l switch to the **crontab** command is short for "list," and it tells you what work you have scheduled for the **cron** process to handle.

Moving On

In this chapter, we've explored some of the different ways to run programs. We've seen ways to run single and multiple programs and move jobs into the background while we go on about our work in the foreground. And, finally, we've looked at some ways to take advantage of UNIX's built-in abilities to schedule jobs for later execution. Now, in the next chapter, we get away from UNIX in its "ugly duckling" role, and look at the X Window System, a graphical user interface (GUI) that will cure you forever of Microsoft Windows envy.

7 Looking Through X Windows

            So far, we've talked about "conventional" UNIX, which is a text-based, command-line interface that only a nerd could love. But in this chapter we explore the X Window System, which has a pretty enough interface to cure you of lusting after Microsoft Windows. More importantly, it takes advantage of the mouse, menu bars, and other features of a graphical user interface to help make you more rather than less productive. For example, you can easily open several windows while you work, as you can see in Figure 7-1.

    A word of disclaimer is in order here as well. You will hear the X Window System referred to variously as X, X Windows, and the X Window System. Well, the last of these three is the official way, but normally people just call it "X" or "X Windows," as we will in this chapter.

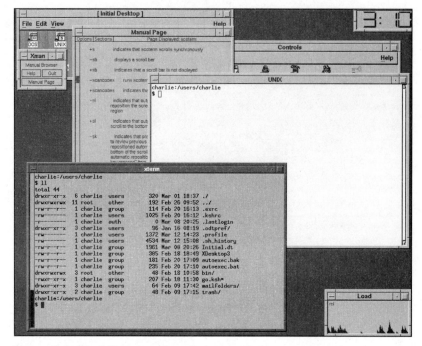

Figure 7-1: *The X Window System lets you have several windows open at the same time.*

The X Window System was originally developed at MIT, and the principal developmental work on it is still carried out there. X has gone through many revisions over the years, and as of this writing is in the version known as "X11R5." Most of what we will discuss here, though, is equally true for X11R4, and in some cases for X11R3 as well. So, even if you are still running on an older version, you should be able to take advantage of many of the same tricks, though the syntax may be a bit different in some cases.

Display Manager Vs. Window Manager

The X Window System is the display manager. By itself, it isn't a very pretty sight. It takes the addition of a window manager to give you the look and feel you expect. All those nice little borders, buttons and mouse tricks are really part of the window manager's job, not the display manager's.

The two most common commercial window managers in the UNIX world are Motif and Open Look. Of the two, Motif seems to be winning the window manager wars, though Sun systems still use Open Look by default. However, even in the Sun world, Motif is available. The window manager allows you to move a window, resize it or shrink it to an icon, or drop down a menu. The display manager (or more properly the X server), on the other hand, directly interacts with the mouse, keyboard and display. The display manager controls fonts, colors and the background screen (the root window). It also is responsible for opening and closing windows and generally managing the resources.

Mousing Around

If you have X Windows running on your UNIX workstation, you undoubtedly know how to use your mouse to click on a window to make it active, and how to move a window around on the screen by clicking and dragging the title bar to the new position. But here are a few other tricks you may not know. (Later in the chapter we will show you a simple way to add items to the popup menu you get when you click your mouse in the root window.)

Tip **Use the mouse to copy text between windows.** If you have two windows open, it's easy to copy text from one window to another. Select the text you want to copy in the first window by positioning the mouse cursor at the beginning of the text you want to copy and pressing down the first mouse button and dragging the cursor over the text you will be copying. The text will now be shown *highlighted* and in reverse. Click on the second window to change the focus to that window, and click the second mouse button. This will insert the highlighted text at the current text cursor position.

Trap **Whenever you're moving or copying text, remember that the mouse cursor and text cursor are not the same.** When you click once, you simply move the mouse cursor to the point where you click.

Tip **Click twice to select an entire word.** When you click twice in quick succession (called a double-click), you will both move the cursor and select or highlight the word at the cursor.

Tip **Triple-click to select an entire line.** Clicking the mouse three times in quick succession highlights an entire line. This is a quick way to transfer a command to another window.

Trap **When you transfer text with the mouse, you transfer it as actual keystrokes.** For example, if you are in **vi,** and you're still in command mode instead of text-insertion mode when you paste the text into the second window, you might actually be passing commands to **vi.**

Tip

Click on the root window to pop up a menu. This menu will let you do a variety of things. You can shuffle your windows up or down to find a window that is buried in a stack of others, open a new window, restart the Motif window manager or just refresh your screen if the graphics have gone haywire. You can take this menu much further, by adding new stuff to it. We'll show you how below in the section called "Customizing Your X."

X Programs You May Already Have

While every vendor's version of the X Window System is just a bit different, most come with a bunch of cool programs—and some that are merely cute without being useful. The ones you are most likely to have are

* **xterm**, a terminal emulation program.
* **xcalc**, a calculator.
* **xclock**, yet another clock program.
* **xman**, a graphical front end to the man pages.
* **xload**, a graphical indicator of the system resource utilization over time.
* **xeyes**, a cute little program that features two eyes that follow your mouse pointer.
* **xlogo**, a totally useless program which displays the X logo.
* **ico**, another cute but useless little program that draws a bouncing icosohedron on your screen.

In addition to these, there are several utilities for manipulating or displaying the properties of the X server. The essential one of these program is, of course, **xterm,** which provides the interface for you to access all of the rest of UNIX.

Xterm Tricks That Make Life Easier

Every version of the X Window System comes with at least the minimum version of Xterm. Plus many vendors include their own custom terminal window that takes advantage of some of the specifics of their system. SCO, for example, includes **scoterm** with their Open Desktop package. HP includes a couple of versions of **hpterm** with their systems—one for their "Visual User Environment" (VUE), an all-encompassing desktop environment based on X, and another for users running only the X Window System. Each of these add specific features that enhance the overall look and feel of the basic Xterm. But we'll stick to the basic Xterm here. Most of the third-party enhanced Xterms accept the same command-line parameters as the basic version, in addition to any other parameters that control the specifics of their own implementation. The result of typing **xterm &** is pretty boring so let's spruce it up. You can control the fonts, colors and all sorts of other stuff.

Tip **Change the colors of xterm to make it easier on the eyes.** Color choice is a very personal, individual thing, but here's a combination that works for us:

```
/usr/bin/X11/xterm -fg white -bg→
    MidnightBlue &
```

This gives you white text on a dark-blue background. Of course, we know someone who finds this way too middle-class and opts for

```
/usr/bin/X11/xterm -fg yellow -bg purple &
```

But then he's on the outer edges of convention.

Tip

To get a list of color possibilities, use showrgb. This will print out a list of colors that are defined in your system. Even if your system doesn't have the **showrgb** program, you can still see this list. Just use **vi** (in its read-only mode, so you don't accidentally mung something) and type in this:

```
view /usr/lib/X11/rgb.txt
```

This will give you a look at the default color database that your system uses. Pick any colors you want from here for your Xterm colors.

Trap

When you type in your Xterm color selections, don't forget to enclose the color name in quotes if the name includes any spaces. A two-word color without quotes will confuse UNIX and cause the command to fail.

Tip

Change the title on your Xterm. You can have your Xterm tell you where you are and who you are logged in as by adding this information to the title bar of the Xterm. The only catch is, this information is static, so if you use the window to log into another, remote machine, it won't be accurate. But we find it useful nonetheless, since it tells us where we started from. Use the **-T** option like this:

```
xterm -T "$(hostname):$LOGNAME — $(date→
  +%X)" &
```

This will put your hostname, login name and time the window was started—all in the title bar.

Tip

Change the font in your Xterm to make it easier to read. The older we get, the bigger the type sizes have to be. We know young programmers who have six or eight Xterm windows open on their screen, each one with tiny little fonts. For them, this may be OK. For ourselves, we like something just a bit larger and easier on the eyes. So we use one of the larger standard fonts for our Xterm:

```
/usr/bin/X11/xterm -fn 10x20 &
```

This makes for a large enough window to actually see what you're doing. Of course, if you're running on a display with a lower resolution than our 1280x1024, or you have good enough eyes and want to squeeze the window size down a bit, try this:

```
/usr/bin/X11/xterm -fn 8x13 &
```

This should give something small enough for most purposes. A good middle choice is the "9x15" font. But examine the other choices on your system. Each vendor's implementation of X includes different fonts, so you may have some additional choices.

Trap

To see which fonts are available, use xlsfonts. But if you run this program with no options specified, you'll have to wait for it to display a complete list of all the fonts available on your system. To limit this list, add the **-fn** *pattern* option to the command line, or pipe the whole thing through **grep** to see a limited list.

Display All Font Characters

To see what a font looks like and what characters are available for it, use **xfd -fn fontname**. This will show you all the characters for that font, as well as give you far more information about each individual character than you are likely to need.

Tip **Add scroll bars to your Xterm to make it easy to scroll back through text.** This will quickly become your standard Xterm. You can add scroll bars to the standard Xterm by using the command-line option **-sb**, which puts a simple scroll bar on the left side of the window, like the one shown in Figure 7-2.

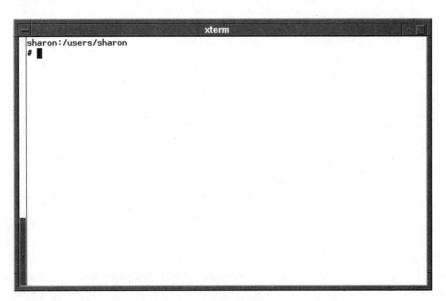

Figure 7-2: Adding scroll bars makes your Xterm more useful.

Enhanced Xterm

Use the enhanced Xterm if your vendor supplies it. Most of the enhanced Xterm versions provide useful additions as well as a slightly different look and feel. But take the same command-line arguments as the default Xterm.

Figure 7-3 shows a typical example of an enhanced Xterm, complete with menus and a right-side scroll bar.

```
                              SCOTerm
 File Edit Options                                              Help
-rw-r--r--    1 root     other     308278 Oct 16  1991 iguana.bmp
drwxr-xr-x    2 root     other         32 Mar 13 09:58 ksh/
drwx------    2 root     other         32 Mar 13 09:58 messages/
-r--r--r--    1 root     other        829 Mar 12 16:23 oldcron.
-r--r--r--    1 root     other        829 Mar 12 16:23 oldcron.0301
-rw-r--r--    1 root     other        829 Mar 12 16:24 oldcron.030153
-rw-r--r--    1 root     other     308278 Oct 07  1991 ripple.bmp
-rw-r--r--    1 root     other         44 Mar 12 16:24 save_msg.dos
-rw-r--r--    1 root     other      32388 Mar 12 16:24 scoimg.gif
drwxr-xr-x    2 root     other         32 Mar 13 09:58 stune.d/
drwxr-xr-x    6 root     other         96 Mar 13 09:58 tar/
-rw-r--r--    1 root     other        113 Mar 12 16:24 tar.log
drwxr-xr-x    2 root     other         32 Mar 13 09:58 test/
-rw-r--r--    1 root     other     448437 Mar 12 16:24 test.xwd
drwxr-xr-x    4 root     other        208 Mar 13 09:58 tmp/
-rw-r--r--    1 root     other       2544 Mar 12 16:24 users.backup.log
drwxr-xr-x    6 root     other         96 Mar 13 09:59 usr/
-rw-r--r--    1 root     other     308278 Oct 16  1991 vangogh.bmp
-rwxr-xr-x    1 root     other      31692 Mar 12 16:24 vdcomp*
-rw-r--r--    1 root     other     308278 Oct 16  1991 volcano.bmp
-rwxr-xr-x    1 root     other      95296 Mar 12 16:24 xcmap*
drwxr-xr-x    2 root     other        192 Mar 13 09:59 xv/
charlie:/work/tmp
#  xwd -frame | xwdtopnm | xv -8 -mono -
```

Figure 7-3: *Use the improved Xterm if your vendor provides one.*

Tip **Make a bigger scroll buffer to use for man pages.**
This is one place where a scroll bar comes in very handy. But the normal wimpy little 64-line scroll bar isn't enough for a lot of man pages. So, with the -sl *nnn* option, crank it up to a full 30 screenfuls, 720 lines. This lets you scroll back and forth even through long **man** pages.

Figure 7-4 shows an example from the Xterm manual.

```
                                    xterm

                window to be repositioned automatically in the normal posi-
                tion at the bottom of the scroll region.

    +sk         This option indicates that pressing a key while using the
                scrollbar should not cause the window to be repositioned.

    -sl number  This option specifies the number of lines to save that have
                been scrolled off the top of the screen.  The default is 64.

    -t          This option indicates that xterm should start in Tektronix
                mode, rather than in VT102 mode.  Switching between the two
                windows is done using the Modes menus.

    +t          This option indicates that xterm should start in VT102 mode.

    -tm string  This option specifies a series of terminal setting keywords
                followed by the characters that should be bound to those
                functions, similar to the stty program.  Allowable keywords
                include: intr, quit, erase, kill, eof, eol, swtch, start,
                stop, brk, susp, dsusp, rprnt, flush, weras, and lnext.  Con-
                trol characters may be specified as ^char (e.g. ^c or ^u) and
                ^? may be used to indicate delete.

    -tn name    This option specifies the name of the terminal type to be set
```

Figure 7-4: *Use a large scroll buffer to view manual pages.*

The Other, Less-impressive X Programs

Along with the essential Xterm come several other useful but more limited X programs, and even some really useless ones. First, the X Calculator, **xcalc**. This is a handy little program that puts a calculator on your screen to help you figure out how you'll spend your future lottery winnings. Obviously, it needs to be able to handle negative numbers. Like all the included X programs, it resides in the **/usr/bin/X11** directory. So if this isn't on your path, you'll want to put it there.

Xcalc

Use xcalc to handle scientific calculations. The Xcalc program has two basic modes. The "normal" mode emulates a TI-30 calculator. This is fine if you like a standard algebraic-mode calculator. But if you want to use the more flexible Reverse Polish Notation that HP made popular, add the **-rpn** command-line option. This result is shown in Figure 7-5.

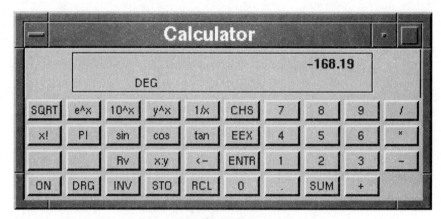

Figure 7-5: *Xcalc can emulate an HP-10 calculator.*

Xload

Use **xload** to monitor your system. This little program gives you a constantly updating display of the amount of system resources you are utilizing. While not directly a measure of cpu usage, once you get used to evaluating it you can get a pretty good idea of exactly how loaded down your system is. Each line of the graph indicates approximately 10 percent usage. But if you find yourself consistently running over two or three lines in the graph, we suggest you find a way to distribute some of the load.

Perhaps a memory increase for the system will lower the number, by reducing the amount of swapping that must occur. In any case, you might like to keep a little Xload graph open down on the corner of the screen. (You can see an example in the lower right corner of the screen in Figure 7-1.) Over time, you'll get a feel for what's normal, and if you suddenly find you're running higher than you would expect, chances are that you should ask your System Administrator to perform whatever incantations seem appropriate.

Xclock

Use the -**geometry** option to control the size and placement of an X program. The Xclock, for example, likes to pop up in the middle of the screen. To put a standard analog clock up in the upper right-hand corner of the screen, try this:

```
xclock -geometry -1+1 &
```

You'll get a nice little clock like the one in Figure 7-6 in the upper right-hand corner of your screen.

Figure 7-6: *The Xclock makes a useful addition to your desktop.*

Xman

Use **xman** to browse for help. The Xman program provides an easy-to-use front end to the manual pages. You find what you need by searching for the specific item or by opening a window, like the one in the figure below, and choosing a volume to look for the manpage in. Once you choose the manual volume, you can easily choose from the list of available commands to view.

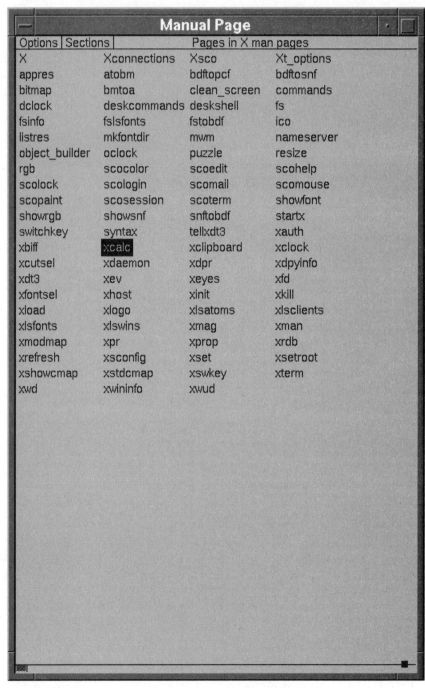

Figure 7-7: Use Xman to find the manual page you need.

The Xman program also makes it easy to browse through the manual page for the command you are interested in, providing a scroll bar on the side, and formatting the page for your display. To find out more about Xman, just use the **xman** command and click on Help. You'll get a useful help screen and you can then choose other pages to get help on by clicking on the Manual Page button.

Less-Useful Programs

But enough about useful programs. Let's talk for a minute about some of the less-practical programs that come with the X Window System. Our favorite little useless one is Xeyes. This does absolutely nothing important. It puts two eyes on your screen, which calmly follow your mouse pointer wherever it goes. See, we told you it was useless. But it is kind of cute, and you might well like to have it open, if only to wow the rubes.

Tip
Try Xeyes for a bit of cute on your desktop. Stick it up in the upper left corner of your screen, and give it some nice blue eyes. If you're the paranoid type, you can think of it as your boss, keeping a watchful eye on you. If you are more the amorous type, you can imagine your sweetie-pie gazing soulfully at you.

```
xeyes -geometry 100x100+0+0 -fg→
    steelblue -center white &
```

The result of this command is shown in Figure 7-8. Well, actually it doesn't really do it justice. You have to see it to believe it.

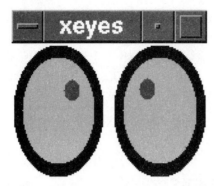

Figure 7-8: *Xeyes follow your mouse, wherever it goes.*

Customizing Your X

The X Window System is a twiddler's dream. You can tweak it
to your heart's content, changing the colors, fonts, appearance,
menus, you name it. All are within the control of you, the user.
There are two basic files—**.Xdefaults** and **.mwmrc**—that you
have control of, and they both reside in your $HOME direc-
tory. The first controls the options and settings for the X server
itself, while the second controls the behavior of the Motif
window manager. You can also add other, task-specific files for
a particular situation. And, finally, each application may have a
special set of defaults that you can set.

The default versions of these files, which should only be
changed by your System Administrator, are kept in the
/usr/lib/X11/app-defaults directory. However, you can
easily copy any of these files to your home directory to give
you a baseline to work from. Some applications will read a
"dotted" version of these files on startup; others prefer that
you include the settings in your **.Xdefaults** file. But in all cases,
you can explicitly load these settings if you want. We strongly
recommend that you do this when first making changes to a
particular set of resources. Then, and only then, if they really
are what you want and what you expected, you can add them
to the default files.

When you first log in to your workstation, these two files are read, and they are not read again unless you explicitly load them. Therefore, any changes you make will not be apparent until then.

Customizing the X Server

The basic X server defaults are just that—pretty basic and bland. But you can easily make changes to the way your desktop looks and behaves by modifying the resource files for either the individual clients or for all clients. The basic syntax of a resource specification is

```
client*resource_name: resource_value
```

Thus you would change the default background color for all your Xterms to LightSteelBlue with the following:

```
XTerm*background:  LightSteelBlue
```

Now, whenever you start an Xterm, if you don't explicitly set the background color on the command line, you will get an Xterm window with a light-steel-blue background. Well, almost. First you have to force your system to read this resource change. We recommend that you put any changes you are trying out into a separate file and that you *not* add them to your **.Xdefaults** file until you are sure they are what you want. We put our changes in a file called **.Xtest** until we're sure they are OK. The command to tell the X server to read this file and incorporate its settings into the X server's database is **xrdb** with the -merge option. So this gives us

```
xrdb -merge ~/.Xtest
```

which will load the **.Xtest** file you just created into your X server's database. Now, try the change you made by starting an

Xterm and see if the background changed. If you didn't muck
up the syntax, all your Xterms should now have a light-blue
background.

Trap **The xrdb command gives you no error messages, but
it is very fussy about exact syntax and even the
presence of trailing white space.** If your changes don't seem
to be working, the two most common problems are leaving out
the colon (:) between the resource and its value, and having a
space or two after the value. This is especially true if you are
converting from X11R4 or earlier to X11R5, since these older
versions of the X server were less punctilious. The latest version
has, for reasons which are clear only to the programmers who
made the change, become intolerant of stray spaces and tabs.

Customizing Your Desktop

Your underlying desktop, or more properly your root window,
is by default an annoying variegated gray color which we find
really hard on the eyes. You can easily fix this, however, using
the **xsetroot** program, which changes the defaults (or restores
them). If you want a solid black background, for example, use

```
xsetroot -solid black
```

which will change the backdrop to solid black. If you want to
try a graph paper look, try this:

```
xsetroot -mod 8 8
```

but we don't think you will stick with that for long. Frankly,
there isn't much that the plain old version of **xsetroot** that

comes with X will do to perk up your background. You can add a bitmap with it, but these aren't nearly as cool as the backgrounds that you can do with Microsoft Windows. There are probably dozens of little utilities out there that will get around this limitation, but one we have used and like is the **xv** program, which is available as shareware from several different sources. The author is John Bradley, and his email address for more information about the program is bradley@cis.upenn.edu. We use it to add **.bmp** or **.gif** files into the root window, resulting in backgrounds that will banish Windows envy quite effectively. The figure below is just one example of the sorts of things you can do, but you are limited only by your imagination and your resourcefulness in finding images.

Figure 7-9: The **Xv** program lets you customize your root window.

Tip **Use the xset program to change font paths, screen saver, and so forth.** Normally you don't need or want to change this stuff, but sometimes you may add a program and it doesn't put its fonts where they belong, or some other problem. Use **xset +fp** *path* to add the new font path to your existing one, and then **xset fp rehash** to make the change actually happen. You can also control the behavior of the built-in screen saver as well as the keyboard and mouse with the **xset** program. For quick command-line help with the program, use **xset -help**, and to see what the current settings are, use **xset -q**.

Customizing Motif

Use the Motif resource file to add features to X. The Motif window manager allows you to add commands to its menus. It even lets you change the behavior of the mouse buttons and keystrokes. We won't go into all the different ways you can do this, or the many different things you can add with this file. But here are some examples of the kinds of things you can do.

But first, a word of caution. Be sure to make a copy of your working configuration before you make changes. Right. Heard that one before, have you?

Trap **Always make a copy of any configuration file before you change it.** Don't say we didn't warn you. Not that we always follow our own advice.

Before you do anything else, copy the default Motif resource file to your home directory. This makes a good starting place to try things:

```
cp /usr/lib/X11/system.mwmrc ~/.mwmrc
cp ~/.mwmrc ~/.mwmrc.original
```

Now you can have an immaculate copy of the current resource file stashed away for safekeeping, and we have a nice starting point for mucking around. Open it up with your favorite text editor (**vi**, of course) and you should see something like Figure 7-10. Depending on your version of Motif and X, the comment character may well be a "#" instead of the "!" you see here.

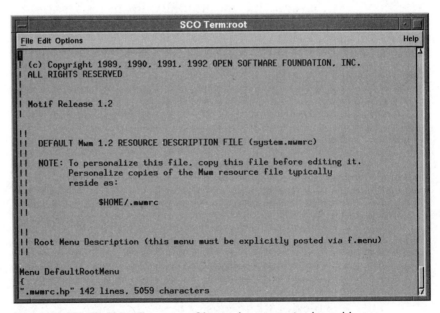

Figure 7-10: *The Motif resource file can be customized to add many additional features.*

Tip

Use the Motif resource file to get help. Let's add the Xman program to our **.mwmrc** file. If you don't have Xman on your system, try the same thing with something else, like Xcalc or even Xeyes!

The resource command to execute a program, whatever it is, is **f.exec.** So let's add the necessary line to our **.mwmrc** file. The syntax is *"label" f.command "options"*. What we want to do is move down to the first section after something that reads sort of like "Menu RootMenu" or some such. Shouldn't be too hard to find. Then add the following line somewhere in the middle of this section:

```
"XMan"      f.exec "xman"
```

Save the file and use the built-in restart command for Motif. Click the mouse in a blank area of the desktop and then select "Restart" from the menu. Confirm that you really want to do this, and Motif will restart. In the process, it will read your changed **.mwmrc** file, and you should now see an option for running Xman on the menu.

Tip

Use f.separator to add lines to your root menu. Add a line with a label of **no-label** and an **f.separator** as the resource command to put a line in the menu. If you include a label of quoted white space and a command of **f.noop**, you will get a blank line in the menu.

The figure below shows a simple set of Motif menu commands, enough to get you started. The possibilities are nearly endless, with menus calling other menus, etc. So have fun.

```
┌──────────────────────────────────────────────────────────────┐
│ —                        SCO Term:root                    ▼ □  │
├──────────────────────────────────────────────────────────────┤
│ File Edit Options                                        Help  │
│ Menu RootMenu                                                  │
│ {                                                              │
│     "Root Menu"        f.title                                 │
│      no-label          f.separator                             │
│      no-label          f.separator                             │
│      "    "            f.noop                                  │
│      no-label          f.separator                             │
│     "XMan"             f.exec "xman "                          │
│      no-label          f.separator                             │
│     "NewWindow"        f.exec "scoterm -fn 10x20 -sb -sl 240"  │
│     "SmallWindow"      f.exec "scoterm -fn 8x13 -sb -sl 240"   │
│     "DOS Window"       f.exec "dos"                            │
│      no-label          f.separator                             │
│     "Shuffle Up"       f.circle_up                             │
│     "Shuffle Down"     f.circle_down                           │
│     "Refresh"          f.refresh                               │
│     no-label           f.separator                             │
│     no-label           f.separator                             │
│     "Desktop"          f.exec "/usr/bin/X11/xdt3"              │
│     no-label           f.separator                             │
│     no-label           f.separator                             │
│     "Restart Mwm"      f.restart                               │
│     "Logout"           f.exec "scosession -stop"               │
│ }                                                              │
└──────────────────────────────────────────────────────────────┘
```

Figure 7-11: *Using the resource file, you can modify your Motif menus to suit yourself.*

Moving On

In this chapter we have covered the starting points for the ways you can take advantage of the X Window System to improve your productivity and increase your fun in UNIX. In the next chapter, we will start to explore some of the small but powerful tools in the UNIX toolbox that can help you build your work environment into a friendly and productive place.

8 The Magic UNIX Toolbox

A UNIX guru is a lot like a millwright with a large box full of tools—each designed for a specific job and each needing the skill and understanding of the user in order to function correctly and efficiently. But most of us are more like the home handyman, struggling along and "making do" with the tools we have. Then every once in a while, after watching too many home improvement shows on TV, we break down and get a new gadget, then struggle to get proficient with it. We know in our hearts that having more tools would make life easier, but we dread taking the time to learn them. In this chapter, we'll take a look at some of the little utility gems that are available in UNIX, so that you can add them to *your* toolbox. We hope this book will give you lots of new tools (without the dread).

Because of its origins as an operating system running on tiny little computers with RAM at a premium, UNIX is composed of hundreds of *small* programs, each one designed to do one or two specific jobs very well then pass on the results to another program that in turn does something else to that data. So in this chapter, we'll look at the great collection of tools available for your toolbox.

Comparison Tools

UNIX has many different ways to compare different things. Many commands, for example, behave like the **find** command. They let you compare against a date or sort by date. Others, like **grep**, let you compare against some *regular expression*. Still others, like **diff**, are strictly about comparing files. Here are our favorites among the comparison tools.

The Grep Family Circus

Grep and its variants are probably the most useful commands in UNIX for comparing and finding text strings. Grep is short for Get Regular ExPression. In most versions of UNIX, Grep comes in three slightly different variations. The regular **grep** lets you search for text that matches a string of text (including wild cards, character sets and metacharacters—which are characters in regular expressions with a special meaning). Then there's **fgrep** (short for Fast grep yet it's actually slower). And finally **egrep** (short for Extended grep) extends the regular expression-matching ability of **grep** and also lets you create logical OR expressions to search for.

There are also some public domain versions of **grep**, each of which has its own peculiarities and advocates, but we'll stick with the standard ones here. And for the most part, we will stick with plain old **grep**.

In its basic form, the syntax of **grep** is this:

```
grep [-options] regexpr [filename(s)]
```

where the options are the following:

-b	Return the block number as well as the matching line.
-c	Return only a count of the number of matching lines.
-h	Return only the matching lines, but not the filenames they were in.
-i	Ignore case when matching.
-l	Return the filenames where there are matches, but not the matching lines.
-n	Return the line numbers in addition to the matching line.
-s	Suppress error messages.
-v	Return only lines which don't match the regular expression.
-w	Matches only whole words. (Not available in all versions of grep).

Of these, the most useful are the -i option to ignore case, and the -v option to reverse the search and return nonmatching lines.

Tip **Use grep -v to find files that don't belong to you.** Here's a quick way to find out if anyone has written files in your home directory that don't belong to you:

```
ls -lA | grep -v "$LOGNAME"
```

This will return a list of only the files in the current directory that are not owned by you. With one exception: it would miss a file that included your login name in the file name even if the file belonged to someone else.

Tip **Use grep -i for case-insensitive searching.** This can be quite handy for making sure that you've been consistent in your text in regard to spelling, style, and so forth. For example, in this book we use the term "System Administrator" as the form for that ultimate of UNIX gods, the Superuser. But we found that we had been inconsistent in capitalization (System/system) and in number, that is, singular/plural (System/Systems). So we used the following to find all of these instances, complete with their line numbers in the file:

```
grep -in "system.* administrator" chp→
  [1- 8].txt
```

which translates to "search chp1.txt through chp8.txt for the string 'system administrator' where the string may be uppercase or lowercase, or any mixture thereof, and where there may or may not be a single character after the 'm' in system."

Trap   **The "." wildcard by itself will fool you!** If we had neglected to put an asterisk after the dot in the above grep expression, it would have missed the times we spelled System without the "s" at the end. But the asterisk said to match zero or more instances of the previous metacharacter.

Tip   **If your version of grep supports the -w option, take advantage of it to match whole words only.** You could, for example, look for all instances of *good* that were used as a whole word by using the regular expression *good*, but this has a problem. What about a sentence that ends with the word *good*? It wouldn't match. We can't use the ".*" trick, since that would match *goody*, and even *goodness*. But if your version of grep will support the -w option, you can use this:

```
grep -iw "good" files
```

which will find all instances of the word "good" but not other words that have "good" buried within them. If your version of **grep** doesn't support this option, by the way, it gets much harder. The following should catch virtually all instances, but we suspect that we will have missed something:

```
grep -i "[\'\"\{\([]good[] \'\",.?!\)\}]"
```

Whew. That seems like just a bit too much work for the result. If your version of **grep** doesn't support the **-w** option, you might want to ask your System Administrator to get a copy of the GNU version of **grep**, which does include this useful option.

What Is a Regular Expression, Anyway?

We've tossed around the term regular expression fairly often throughout this book, and you will continue to see it in any additional UNIX reading you do, including the manpages. A regular expression is a string of characters—which may include wildcards and metacharacters—that's used by one of the text utilities as a search pattern. It looks much like the wildcards used by file utilities, and it includes many of the same special characters. But it's not quite the same.

A regular expression describes the pattern you are looking for. It can include sets of characters such as [aA] (which would match both uppercase and lowercase instances of "A"); or a wildcard like "*" (which matches any number of characters, including zero, but not special characters) or "." (which matches any single character). Two other useful metacharacters are ^ and $, which match the beginning and end of the line, respectively.

A complete description of regular expressions is way beyond the scope of this book, but you can find highly specialized books on UNIX tools, and most UNIX manuals also include good descriptions.

File Comparisons

UNIX provides several file comparison tools. You can compare two or even three different text files, compare binary files, or take a file that has been sorted and remove duplicate lines from it.

Tip **Use diff to compare two text files.** This is the one you will probably use the most often. Its syntax is simple, but reading its output can be a bit annoying. The syntax is this:

```
diff [options] file1 file2
```

These are the options:

* -b Ignore repeating white space.
* -e Create a command script that can be fed to the **ed** editor to recreate file2 from file1.
* -f Create a script to recreate file1 from file2.
* -h Fast, but less rigorous. Disables -e and -f options.

If the two files are pretty similar, this can be a useful way to check to see what has changed. Redirect the output from **diff -e** to a log file, and you can see what was changed in the file and decide if that change was appropriate.

Tip **Use diff3 to compare three similar files to find differences.** The resulting output lets you see what has changed and in which file it has changed. You can actually do a pretty decent version-control system based on this command.

Tip **Use the cmp command to compare binary files.**
This command lets you see if two apparently identical files
actually are. Useful if the file sizes are the same but you think
someone has accidentally changed one. When used with the -s
option, you get back simply an exit code: 0 if they are the
same, 1 if they are different and 2 if one or both of the files
were inaccessible.

Text-Manipulating Tools

The tool set to view and manipulate text files is enormous in
UNIX, but here are some of our favorites. They include tools
to view an entire file, view the beginning and end of a file, sort
the file and check the spelling of the file. In earlier chapters,
we've already seen ways to quickly reformat a file for printing
with the **pr** command (Chapter 5). In Chapter 3 we looked at
vi as a tool to edit text files, along with brief looks at some of
the other text-editing tools available.

Tip **Use more to page through a file once.** The **more**
command lets you look through a file one page at a time. You
can use */regexp* to jump ahead in the file by searching for the
regular expression, but you can't go backward. There are
other, more flexible paging programs around, however, so if
you find yourself frustrated by the limitation of **more**, ask your
System Administrator to get a copy of **less** for your system.
This little program lets you page back and forth through the
file and is quite a bit handier than **more**. Or, get in the habit of
using **vi** in its read only form, **view**, as a substitute.

Tip

Pipe the output of long directory listings to more to prevent them from scrolling off the screen. Once you get in the habit of using **ls -lAF** as your directory-listing command, it's hard to give up all that extra information. This is why we suggested you make a simple alias out of it to **ll** (for Long Listing). But the down side is that it is much more likely to scroll off the screen than a simple **ls** would be. So, pipe the result to more, and you'll be able to see your listing a page at a time **ll | more**.

Tip

Use head to see just the beginning of a file. Most versions of UNIX come with a program called **head** which can show you just the first few lines of a file (or of standard input if you are piping something to it). You can control the number of lines shown by using the *-nn* option on the command line, where *nn* is the number of lines to show. The default is usually 10. This command is extremely useful if for example you are looking for a particular file and can't remember its exact name, but you *do* remember a particular phrase in the file's header. If it's one of several files that end in **.ksh**, then try this command to find the file you want:

```
head *.ksh | more
```

This will show you the first ten lines of each file, complete with a one-line header to give you the file name. Figure 8-1 shows a typical result.

```
┌─────────────────────────────────────────────────────────────────┐
│  ─                        SCOTerm:charlie                   ▪ │□│ │
├─────────────────────────────────────────────────────────────────┤
│  File Edit Options                                          Help │
│ ==> archive.ksh <==                                            ▲ │
│ #!/bin/ksh                                                       │
│ #=============================================================   │
│ #                                                                │
│ # Filename: archive.ksh                                          │
│ #                                                                │
│ #  Shell script to save the the old database dumps to tape       │
│ #   (/dev/dat) for long term storage. Cleans up the old dumps,   │
│ #   leaving only the last two on the hard disk.                  │
│ #                                                                │
│ #      Created: 6/9/94 by slc                                    │
│                                                                  │
│ ==> dump.ksh <==                                                 │
│ #!/bin/ksh                                                       │
│ #=============================================================   │
│ #                                                                │
│ # Filename: dump.ksh                                             │
│ #                                                                │
│ #  Shell script to dump the database to secondary disk storage   │
│ #   for safe keeping. Just in case.                              │
│ #                                                                │
│ #      Created: 6/3/94 by cpr                                    │
│ #                                                                │
│ charlie:/users/charlie/bin                                       │
│ $ ▮                                                            ▽ │
└─────────────────────────────────────────────────────────────────┘
```

Figure 8-1: *Use **head** to find the file you need.*

Tip

Use head to find the files that have changed recently.
You know the file you want is in the directory somewhere. You
just worked on it yesterday, so it should be one of the first files
in the list if you sort your listing by date. Try this:

```
ls -tlA | head -20
```

to see just the last 20 files that have been modified.

Tip

Use tail to see the end of a file. The tail command
works exactly like the **head** command, except that it shows you
the end of the file, not the beginning. This makes it extremely
useful for looking at things like **log** files that grow over time.
You don't want to have to read through the whole file to see
what's happened; you just want to see the last few lines to find

out if there are any recent changes. Since all the changes will be at the end of the file, **tail** is perfect for this.

Tip 77 Use the tee command to send output to both a file and your terminal. We always use this one when we're running full backups. The output goes to a log file, just in case we want to check later, but it's nice to have the output going to the screen as well. That way, you can be doing something else and just glance over to the screen periodically to see how the process is going. For example, you might do a backup with a command like this:

```
tar -cvf /dev/dat ~ | tee -a /tmp/bkup.log
```

The **-a** in the command tells **tee** to append its output to the file, not overwrite it.

Tip 77 Use spell to check the spelling of your files. UNIX comes with its own built-in spell checker. Just take any text file and run the spell command on it, and UNIX will tell you which words it thinks are misspelled. The syntax is:

```
spell [options] [files]
```

The most useful of the options is **+***wordlist* where *wordlist* is a file containing a user dictionary of words not included in the main dictionary. A useful way to set this up is to create a special dictionary for a given project that might have some specialized words or jargon used with it. Then keep that word list in the home directory of the project. You can even have an environment variable point to it, so that it's easy to change or update your scripts.

Tip **Use spell twice to create a custom dictionary.** Here's an easy way to create that custom dictionary. Run spell twice. The first time, use something like this:

```
spell project.doc > words.special
```

The document you're checking is *project.doc* and the output of the spellcheck is being directed to your own custom directory, called *words.special* in this example. After you run the spell program, edit the file **words.special** to remove any actually misspelled words. But leave in the jargon or other specialized terms you're using in your project. Now you have a custom dictionary for the project. Run the rest of your project files through spell to search for misspelled words:

```
spell +words.special proj*.doc > words.wrong
```

Now you have the *actual* misspellings (that don't include your specialized terms) in the file **words.wrong**. You can use your editor (**vi**, we hope) to search files for words that are in **words.wrong**. You'll be able to find and correct actual misspellings without being continually asked about your specialized words.

Tip **Use sort to create a sorted file.** UNIX comes with its own **sort** command. By default, it is case-sensitive, but you can easily turn that off with the **-f** option. Sort can be used to sort output by the beginning of each line (the default) or by any field within the line, where fields are separated by either white space (tab or space, the default) or some other, specified character. So, to sort the **/etc/password** file, by group, this is what you would use:

```
sort +3n -t: /etc/passwd > /tmp/
sorted.passwd
```

This says to sort the file by the fourth field (starts counting at 0), use a delimiter between fields of ":", and send the output to the file **/tmp/sorted.passwd**.

Tip

Use the tr command to clean up mixed-case files.
The translate utility, **tr**, is a handy little command that takes input and converts all the characters in one character set to the matching characters in another character set. Probably its most common use is to convert a file or command to all-uppercase or all-lowercase. For example, to convert a file that is mixed uppercase and lowercase to all-uppercase, try the following:

```
cat mixed.case | tr "[a-z]" "[A-Z]" > /→
    tmp/upper.case
```

This takes every instance of a letter in the first set of characters "[a-z]" and converts them to the corresponding character in the second set, "[A-Z]". Note that this command is no smarter than you might expect. It knows absolutely nothing about the two strings you give it, except that they are the same length. So, here is an easy way to do a *very* simple encryption of a file:

```
cat file | tr "[a-z]" "[A-Z]" | tr "[A-Z]"→
    "[B-Z]A" > file.shifted
```

Of course, it wouldn't take a cryptographer longer than a few minutes to figure out that you'd shifted each letter one position. But it's probably not professional cryptographers who are peering at your files when they shouldn't. This is an easy way to do encryption, and it's even easier to undo when you want to read the file.

```
cat file.shifted | tr "[B-Z]A" "[A-Z]" >→
   file.unshifted
```

But if your needs for security are more serious than just keeping nosy eyes away from a sensitive file, you will want to use the **crypt** command discussed below under "Miscellaneous Tools."

Miscellaneous Tools

Here are some assorted goodies that didn't seem to fit anywhere else and yet are too valuable to leave out. First, some file-manipulation tools.

Tip **Use compress to shrink the size of a file.** This gem can save you tons of disk space for files you don't use very often but need to keep available on disk. Just compress them, and when you need them for something, use the uncompress option. Compressed files have a file name that ends in **.Z** and they can take up significantly less space, depending on the type of file. For example, TIFF graphic files will compress to about 5 percent of their original size, and our daily database exports compress to about 25 percent of their original bulk. The amount of compression for other files will vary widely. Text files compress nicely; program files compress hardly at all. To compress a file, use **compress** *filenames*. To uncompress them, use **uncompress** *filenames* or **compress -d** *filenames*. Both are the same, and both assume that the file to be uncompressed ends in **.Z** so you don't need to add that to the command line.

Tip
To encrypt a file to prevent prying eyes from being able to read it, use the crypt command. This command is based on the famous Enigma encoding machine developed in Germany but with a 256-element "wheel." As such, it can be broken, but not easily and not without a substantial amount of computing time and power, especially if the password used is not short. The **crypt** command is not available on versions of UNIX shipped outside the US due to export restrictions. In fact, it may not even be on the shipped version you receive in the US, unless you specifically request it. If you have it, it'll provide a high level of security. The **crypt** command has the syntax **crypt [password]** < *infile* > *outfile*.

Tip
Use the cal program to print a quick calendar. This little prize produces, with no options, either a three-month calendar across your screen or a one-month or one-year calendar depending on what you ask for. The result of **cal** and **cal june** are shown in Figure 8-2.

```
┌─                          SCOTerm:charlie                         · □
 File Edit Options                                                    Help
 charlie:/users/charlie
 $ cal june 1994
     June 1994
  S  M Tu  W Th  F  S
           1  2  3  4
  5  6  7  8  9 10 11
 12 13 14 15 16 17 18
 19 20 21 22 23 24 25
 26 27 28 29 30

 charlie:/users/charlie
 $ cal
 Sun Mar 20 16:35:21 1994
         Feb                   Mar                   Apr
  S  M Tu  W Th  F  S    S  M Tu  W Th  F  S    S  M Tu  W Th  F  S
        1  2  3  4  5          1  2  3  4  5                   1  2
  6  7  8  9 10 11 12    6  7  8  9 10 11 12    3  4  5  6  7  8  9
 13 14 15 16 17 18 19   13 14 15 16 17 18 19   10 11 12 13 14 15 16
 20 21 22 23 24 25 26   20 21 22 23 24 25 26   17 18 19 20 21 22 23
 27 28                  27 28 29 30 31         24 25 26 27 28 29 30

 charlie:/users/charlie
 $ █
```

Figure 8-2: *The **cal** program gives a useful little calendar when you need it.*

Tip 77

Use the calendar program to create a tickler file.

Actually, you create the tickler file with **vi** or your favorite
editor; it should have the format **date event-description** where
each event is on a single line and the dates are in some sort of
reasonable form that the calendar can interpret. Then, add the
command to your **.profile** so that you are reminded every time
you log in of the event schedule for that day and the next. You
can even add it to your **crontab** or as an **at** command. Then,
you get periodically reminded of the things you need to do
today. The result is like Figure 8-3.

```
┌─────────────────────────────── XTerm ───────────────────────────┐
│ /users/sharon                                                    │
│ $ calendar                                                       │
│ 3/20    Meet w/ Dale about progress of new PI program. Must be completed by 4/1│
│ 3/20    3pm - New Model Meeting - ALL HANDS!                     │
│ March 21 Call FedEx for pickup                                   │
│ 3/21    Call Harry - see if he has any free basketball tickets!  │
│ /users/sharon                                                    │
│ $ █                                                              │
│                                                                  │
│                                                                  │
│                                                                  │
│                                                                  │
│                                                                  │
│                                                                  │
│                                                                  │
└──────────────────────────────────────────────────────────────────┘
```

Figure 8-3: *Use **calendar** to remind yourself of important events.*

Moving On

In this chapter, we have explored some of the tools in the UNIX toolbox, but these are just the proverbial tip of the iceberg. Use these tips as a start on your road to discovery. There are many more programs out there we haven't even touched on, and lots more ways to use the ones we have. In the next chapter, we will learn about the tricks and traps of connecting your computer to the larger world. First we'll investigate some useful commands for your local network, and then look at some that will help you start the journey to explore the much larger outside network.

9 Connecting to Others

Working on your single workstation or terminal is nice, but it isn't really what UNIX is all about. UNIX has been and will continue to be primarily a networked operating system. And this means some changes in thinking and behavior for those of us brought up in the single-tasking, single-user DOS environment. In this chapter we will explore some of the features and foibles of connecting to other computers within a workgroup, and reaching out to the wider world of the Internet. For much, much more about the Internet and how to take advantage of it, you really should get a copy of Ventana Press's *Internet Tour Guide* (available in Mac, PC and Windows editions).

We'll start this chapter by looking at tools you would use in a local network, along with tools that are primarily designed for bigger and more diverse networks, including the Internet. But it's important to remember that many of these tools actually work across a broad range of network situations and perform equally well from a dial-up modem connection or a high-speed fiber-optic network. Of course, the speed of the response will be just a bit different, but let's not dwell on that.

Reach Out & Touch Someone

When you work in a local network, there are lots of ways you can take advantage of the distributed nature of the UNIX networking environment. Some UNIX systems have one large central server, much like a PC network. But others use multiple, smaller workstations. Both work, and, if set up properly, look very much the same to their users. But there are some important differences. If you have, for example, a large central server, with terminals located at each desk, then the concept of copying files from machine to machine makes little or no sense, since they're all stored on a central machine. But if you are working in a distributed environment—with multiple workstations, each of which may be the server for a different program or function—then the time will come when you'll need to copy files to other machines in order to share them around. Even here, though, much of this should be handled transparently, usually with a common $HOME directory structure.

We'll look at this local situation as if it were a distributed workstation environment. That is, it might consist of multiple workstations, each with its own hard disk and processor. It might have some workstations without hard disks. Or it might even have simple terminals or Xterminals. But don't worry if you are in a situation with one big central server and only terminals or Xterminals. Most of this will still apply to you. And if it doesn't, just skip over that part.

Sharing Files in Your Workgroup

Probably the single most common need in a local network environment is the ability to share files with others in the workgroup. UNIX makes this simple. We've actually already touched on some of the tricks to do this, but here we want to pull all that together. You may well need the help of your

System Administrator to set up the initial group and directory structure. But once you get it all set up, you should be able to handle your files comfortably within your own group.

Tip

Designate one person in your workgroup as a local System Administrator. To distinguish this person from the main System Administrator, let's call him or her the Project Manager. And, by the way, usually the best person to designate for this position is the actual project manager or team leader for your group. Usually this person will be able to handle many of the same functions as the main System Administrator. The Project Manager will be the owner of the main files and directories the group uses, and will be the contact point between the workgroup and the System Administrator. Then the System Administrator won't have to be constantly tweaking permissions, ownerships and such stuff for the group, and that august (and usually seriously overworked) individual will probably be even more willing to give help when it's needed. But more important, it means that most of the time the workgroup can handle its own day-to-day operations without waiting in the System Administrator's priority queue to get something taken care of.

The idea here is that the Project Manager owns all directories and "core" files for the group. Everyone in the group shares a special group id. Templates and standards are created for the group's work. The templates are read-only for the group members and read/write for the Project Manager. If changes are needed in a core file, the Project Manager makes the change and makes it available for all the others in the group. This is an excellent way to maintain standard forms throughout a group.

The other files that the Project Manager must worry about are resource files. These could be X or Motif resources, to ensure that standard buttons and styles, including fonts and colors, are used in a programming project. They also might include a standard set of **vi** macros that everyone uses, or just the environment variables that control locations of files and inclusions.

Tip   **Use NFS mounting to make the workgroup's directory local.** This will require the initial intervention of the System Administrator to set everything up, but once established will allow the members of the workgroup to work on different machines without being logged into one single machine. There are several hidden benefits in this arrangement. Each person in the workgroup can arrange their workstation as they wish, yet files, scripts, and so forth, that are common to the group all appear in the same relative place for everyone in the group. A second benefit is that the processing load is spread across multiple machines, so the system won't become loaded down unduly when everyone is working on the same project at the same time. The catch to this, of course, is that you may need multiple versions of any specialized software you are using. If it's all located on only one machine, that machine still ends up doing all the processing.

Communicating Within Your Group

UNIX provides several tools for handling communications within your local network or workgroup. These range from the simple **ping** that lets you know if a machine is connected, to commands like **talk** that let you carry on a conversation with another user on the network, to the various and sundry electronic mail programs that let you send email to your workgroup and beyond.

Tip
77 **Use ping to find out which machines are available.**
The **ping** program is probably the most basic UNIX network-ing command. It simply sends a tiny little packet to the address you tell it then listens to see if the other machine "echos" back the packet. You can use the machine's Internet address, which looks something like **192.78.222.81**, or you can use the machine's _name,_ as in

```
ping rci1
```

The name will be the name in either your local **hosts** file or as resolved by the network nameserver. But in any case it will be the name the network expects to use to find a particular machine. The result of ping will look something like what you see in Figure 9-1.

If a machine doesn't respond to **ping**, then it isn't going to respond to anything else, because the network simply can't see it. Time to make an offering to the System Administrator (chocolates are nice), unless the reason for the problem is simple and obvious—for example, the machine is turned off. In which case, the System Administrator is already involved be-cause rebooting a UNIX machine is not as simple as rebooting a DOS machine.

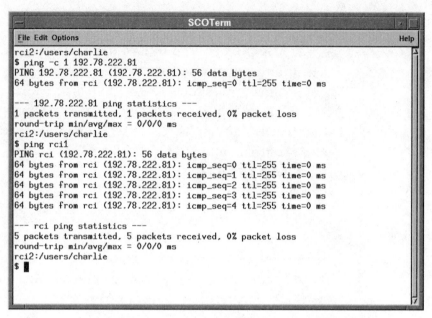

```
                              SCOTerm
  File Edit Options                                              Help
  rci2:/users/charlie
  $ ping -c 1 192.78.222.81
  PING 192.78.222.81 (192.78.222.81): 56 data bytes
  64 bytes from rci (192.78.222.81): icmp_seq=0 ttl=255 time=0 ms

  --- 192.78.222.81 ping statistics ---
  1 packets transmitted, 1 packets received, 0% packet loss
  round-trip min/avg/max = 0/0/0 ms
  rci2:/users/charlie
  $ ping rci1
  PING rci (192.78.222.81): 56 data bytes
  64 bytes from rci (192.78.222.81): icmp_seq=0 ttl=255 time=0 ms
  64 bytes from rci (192.78.222.81): icmp_seq=1 ttl=255 time=0 ms
  64 bytes from rci (192.78.222.81): icmp_seq=2 ttl=255 time=0 ms
  64 bytes from rci (192.78.222.81): icmp_seq=3 ttl=255 time=0 ms
  64 bytes from rci (192.78.222.81): icmp_seq=4 ttl=255 time=0 ms

  --- rci ping statistics ---
  5 packets transmitted, 5 packets received, 0% packet loss
  round-trip min/avg/max = 0/0/0 ms
  rci2:/users/charlie
  $ ▮
```

Figure 9-1: *The **ping** program is used to find out if a machine is on the network.*

Tip

Use write to send a quick message to another user logged into your machine. The **write** command is perfect for sending a quick message to another user who is either on a terminal connected to your workstation or remotely logged in to it. For example, you can easily send a message to the project manager who is remotely logged in to your workstation with

```
write yasminek
```

She would respond with a similar **write** command to you. You could then suggest a meeting, or whatever. When you were done, the command would terminate when you sent an End Of File (EOF) character, usually a Ctrl-D.

The write command writes directly to the terminal.
This can cause some programs, such as **vi**, to go quietly
(or not so quietly) nuts. Before you get in the habit of using
write or any command that writes directly to someone else's
display, you should have a clear agreement that this is or is not
acceptable behavior.

**Use mesg n to turn off write permission to your
terminal.** This protects you from having people sendmessages
to you while you are working with something like **vi** which
might not like it. To re-enable message writing to your terminal, use **mesg y** and others will again be able to write to your
terminal.

**If you are using X Windows, keep one XTerm window
just for write conversations.** When you're in a workgroup
and want to be able to send messages back and forth without
causing problems, you can designate a specific window for
"chatting" with each other. We like to use **ttyp1** as our chat
window. We keep it open but in the background. When a
message comes in to that window, we get a beep and we just
click on the window to pop it up to the top.

**The talk command lets you chat with another user in
your workgroup, even if that other user is on a
different machine.** (The **talk** command also writes directly to
your screen, but it will split the screen into two separate
halves—one for what you are writing and one for what is being
sent to you by the other user.) But it's even more important
than it is with the **write** command that the person receiving

the request to talk isn't in the middle of something else. To chat with another user, the syntax is

```
talk username@hostname
```

where *username* is their login name, and *hostname* is their machine's name as defined in the **hosts** table.

The Wall

Use the **wall** command to send a message to everyone who is logged into your computer. It won't cross over to other machines, so you can't really use it to send a message to everyone on the network. In a traditional UNIX environment, with a single large server and lots of terminals off of it, this works perfectly. But in today's distributed workstation environment, you'll have to use one of the mail commands to reach everyone in your workgroup.

Who, What, When, Why & Where

When you work in a distributed environment, you often forget that you're not the only person using your workstation. After all, it looks sort of like a PC, with its little pizza-box style and everything right there on your desk. So you work along, and suddenly you notice that your hard disk is thrashing around, your keyboard response has gotten really slow, and it feels like you're trying to run in hip-deep water. How could this be? Well, someone out there is using your machine to do a pretty intensive task, and they didn't think about the consequences to you. Maybe they just started a major compile which led to a core dump. So, how to find the culprit?

Tip

Use the who command to see who is logged in to your workstation. This command, which has lots of other options, in its simplest form is the ideal way to find out who is logged in to your computer. The result is shown in Figure 9-2.

```
┌─────────────────────────── SCO Term ───────────────────────────┐
│ File Edit Options                                          Help │
├─────────────────────────────────────────────────────────────────┤
│ rci:/ $ who                                                      │
│ root         tty02       Mar 25 06:13                            │
│ root         ttyp0       Mar 25 06:14                            │
│ root         ttyp2       Mar 25 06:14                            │
│ root         ttyp1       Mar 25 06:14                            │
│ root         ttyp3       Mar 25 06:14                            │
│ root         ttyp4       Mar 25 06:14                            │
│ harold       ttyp5       Mar 25 08:01                            │
│ sharon       ttyp6       Mar 25 08:01                            │
│ root         ttyp7       Mar 25 08:04                            │
│ rci:/ $ █                                                        │
└─────────────────────────────────────────────────────────────────┘
```

Figure 9-2: Use **who** to see who is logged into your computer.

The **who** command has lots of other options, mostly of interest to System Administrators, but one option you might find useful is -**a** (for *all*). The output from this command may give you a bit more information than you really want. But if you combine it with -**H** (so you get headings to tell you what column is what) you can pick out the information you want. Figure 9-3 shows the output of the **who -aH** command.

```
┌─────────────────────────────────────────────────────────────────────────┐
│─                              SCO Term:root                            · □│
├─────────────────────────────────────────────────────────────────────────┤
│ File Edit Options                                                    Help │
│ $ who -aH | more                                                        ▲ │
│ NAME       LINE        TIME          IDLE  PID  COMMENTS                  │
│  .         system boot Mar 24 13:06                                      │
│  .         run-level 2 Mar 24 13:06    2    0   S                        │
│ asktimer   .           Mar 24 14:41  old   34  id=ck term=0   exit=1     │
│  .         old time    Mar 24 14:39    0                                 │
│  .         new time    Mar 24 14:41    0                                 │
│ docpyrt    .           Mar 24 14:41  old   43  id=copy term=0  exit=0    │
│ brc        .           Mar 24 14:41  old   48  id=brc term=0   exit=0    │
│ brc        .           Mar 24 14:41  old   52  id=mt term=0    exit=0    │
│ scologin   .           Mar 24 14:41  old   56  id=sclb term=0  exit=0    │
│ authckrc   .           Mar 24 14:41  old   67  id=ack term=0   exit=2    │
│ rc2        .           Mar 24 14:41  old  107  id=r2 term=0    exit=0    │
│ LOGIN      tty01       Mar 24 14:41  0:12  405                           │
│ LOGIN      tty03       Mar 24 14:41  0:12  406                           │
│ LOGIN      tty04       Mar 24 14:41  0:12  407                           │
│ LOGIN      tty05       Mar 24 14:41  0:12  408                           │
│ LOGIN      tty06       Mar 24 14:41  0:12  409                           │
│ LOGIN      tty07       Mar 24 14:41  0:12  410                           │
│ LOGIN      tty08       Mar 24 14:41  0:12  411                           │
│ LOGIN      tty09       Mar 24 14:41  0:12  418                           │
│ LOGIN      tty10       Mar 24 14:41  0:12  420                           │
│ LOGIN      tty11       Mar 24 14:41  0:12  422                           │
│ LOGIN      tty12       Mar 24 14:41  0:12  427                           │
│ --More--                                                                 │
└─────────────────────────────────────────────────────────────────────────┘
```

Figure 9-3: *The **who -aH** command tells you who's on the system and what's going on.*

Tip

To solve an identity crisis, use the who am i command. With this command, if you have more than one account on a system or are using a shared account for a project, you can find out who the system thinks you are and which terminal or pseudo-terminal you are logged in on. And yes, you really do type it as three separate words—probably the only such command in the entire UNIX command set. Some systems also support a different version of this command: **whoami,** all as a single word. If yours does, this can be useful to find out what account you are actually logged into right now.

Use who -f to get just the real logins. This option strips out any pseudo-terminals that would be included in the command, giving you a list of only actual logins. If you are running the X Window System, this can be a more meaningful result.

Use finger to find out more information about the people on your machine. This command, which isn't supported on all versions of UNIX, tells you not only about the people who are logged in to your machine but how long they have been active on your system, their real names, and all sorts of other stuff as well. You can also use this in a network to get information about other people not currently logged in.

Use the hostname command to find out where you are. If you work in a distributed environment and you often have to log into other machines, it can be a nuisance to keep track of which machine you're on at any point. This is especially true if you're working in X Windows, with several different terminal windows open. So, to find out where you are (if you find yourself doing this a lot), add **hostname** to your prompt by putting a pair of lines in your **.profile**, like this:

```
host=$(hostname)
PS1='${host%%.*}:$PWD \$ '
```

You'll get a prompt like this:

```
rci:/users/sharon $
```

which provides a constant reminder. If you like multiple-line prompts, just insert a ^J into the string in front of the \$ and you will get a nice two-line version of the prompt.

Tip **Use mail or one of the many improved versions of it to communicate with your workgroup.** Actually **mail** makes it almost as easy to communicate with your friends across the world as it is to communicate with a coworker in the next office. There are almost as many different improved versions of the basic **mail** program as there are versions of UNIX. But a widely available, easy-to-use version that supports both text modes and graphics modes and works on virtually any system is the **elm** package. Written by Dave Taylor, this program is in the public domain (in other words, it's not copyrighted or licensed, so you don't have to pay for it). If the mail package you have is hard to use, ask your System Administrator to get a copy of **elm**. Everyone will be happier. It's available from a variety of anonymous ftp sites (more on what that means shortly), including tut.cis.ohio-state.edu.

The r Commands

The **r remote** commands make life much easier on a local network. Plus, they provide some useful tricks on your own local machine since they include some options that the more traditional commands sometimes lack. The commands in this group are

* rcp   The remote version of the **cp** command.
* rlogin Logs into another machine.
* rcmd   Executes a command remotely.
* rsh   Same as rcmd on systems where it exists.

These commands make it simple and easy to move around, execute programs and manipulate files in a distributed environment. On many systems, the **rsh** command is reserved for a restricted form of the Bourne shell, and on these systems the command is called **rcmd**. But in either case, they allow you to open a shell on a remote system and execute a series of commands that are then displayed on your system. The **rlogin** command allows you to log into the remote machine and execute commands just as if you were sitting at a terminal connected to it. And the **rcp** command allows you to copy files or whole directory structures between machines.

Tip **Use rlogin to work interactively on another machine.** This command is perfect when you want to work on the other machine just as if it were your own workstation. The syntax is

```
rlogin remotehost [-l username]
```

Depending on how the System Administrator has set up permissions, you may not even need to give a password on the remote machine. And if you have to do this often and have accounts on both machines, you can (and should) create a **.rhosts** file on both machines that allows you to log in without a password. Your account on the remote machine doesn't even have to have the same username, so long as the **.rhosts** file is set correctly. This file should have lines of this form:

```
hostname username
```

where the hostname is the actual hostname as given in /etc/hosts, not an alias, and the username field is the actual user's login name on the remote machine.

Tip

Use rlogin to your own machine as a safety check when you make changes to your configuration. This single trick will save you offerings on the System Administrator's altar if you just remember to do it *before* you log off. By doing (or attempting to do) a remote login to your own machine, you will force a new read of your configuration files. This allows you to test those changes you just put in, without logging all the way out. This way, if you did something really fatal, you can just back out and restore the saved version you made first. You did make a copy before you started, didn't you?

Tip

Use rcmd or rsh, whichever is on your system, to run a single program on another machine. This command is the one to use when you want to launch a program or script on another machine but you don't need to actually work with multiple programs on that machine. Here you must have an equivalency set up using **.rhosts** on the remote machine, since you can't be prompted for a password. This command has the following syntax:

```
rcmd [-1 username] hostname command
```

If this program is known as **rsh** or **remsh** on your system, then substitute the appropriate command. In any case, they all work essentially the same, and all have the same pitfalls. Because they don't prompt for a password, they can constitute a potential security problem if the program they are running on the remote machine allows the user to shell out from the program. Further, it can be tricky to set up these commands, since in some cases errors are not necessarily passed back through to you but are eaten by the spawned shell on the remote machine. But they do have the advantage of simplicity once they are set up. You can include the commands inside a shell script then make that shell script available to all users in your workgroup. They don't have to know anything about the nitty gritty details of how it works; all they need to know is that when they type **wp** they will start WordPerfect to edit the documents they're working on, even though the WordPerfect server isn't their machine at all.

Tip **Use the rcp command to copy files and directories from one machine to another.** Within a local network, this is far and away the easiest way to move files around. The syntax is similar to the familiar **cp** command, but now you need to add a machine name for the remote machine. So the command will have this syntax:

```
rcp [options] remotehost:sourcefile→
  localfile
rcp [options] remotehost:sourcefiles→
  localdirectory
```

where the remote and local side of the command can be reversed. The options available are -**p**, which preserves the times and permissions of the remote files, and -**r**, which copies recursively down the directory structure below the starting remote directory. The -**r** is a powerful addition that allows you to copy entire directory structures with a single command, but not all versions of the regular **cp** command support it.

Tip **Use rcp -rp to copy an entire directory structure on your local machine even if your version of cp doesn't support recursive copies.** Some versions of UNIX *still* don't support a smarter and more powerful version of the **cp** command that will handle recursive copies. But even these support it for remote copying, so you'll just have to cheat! Use **rcp** within your own machine but treat one side of the command as if your local machine were in fact a remote one. To copy the **/tmp/local/bin** directory, and all the directories under it, to **/usr/local/bin** on your own machine, use this:

```
rcp -rp localhost:/tmp/local/bin /usr/→
   local/bin
```

Voila! Maybe someday soon your UNIX vendor will get with the program and make this workaround unnecessary. But in the meantime, you have a way to get the job done. This even works when a **mv** won't work because you would be crossing file systems.

Connecting to the Larger World

There is a huge range of commands that can connect your computer to the outside world—too many to mention them all here. Some of them are thankfully finally going the way of the dodo bird, since they had a complexity and user-friendliness level that even a confirmed nerd couldn't love. But there are two you will want to know about that you may well use even in a local network situation: the **telnet** and the **ftp** commands. These two open up a whole new world of possibilities for connecting to the Internet, browsing its files and making news groups friendlier and more accessible.

The ftp File Transfer Protocol

If you have to transfer files between different machines running different operating systems (such as from a UNIX machine to a DOS PC), then the chances are that your best bet is **ftp**, which is supported on a broad range of platforms and operating systems. We won't go into all the different commands that **ftp** supports or all the ways it can be used, but a typical **ftp** session might go something like this.

1. You start by typing **ftp** on the command line. At this point, you can add the hostname of the machine you want to initially connect to. The available options are

    -d Enable debugging mode.

    -g Disable filename globbing.

    -i Disable interactive prompting.

    -n Don't automatically login upon initial connection.

    -v Verbose - show additional information about what is happening.

    -t Turn on packet tracing.

2. Then you connect to the remote site using **open host,** where host may be a simple local hostname or a fully qualified hostname if you are attempting to connect to a remote machine.

3. You're prompted for an account and a password on the remote system. If you are out on the Internet trying to get a file someone told you about, and you don't have an account on the remote machine, use **anonymous** as the user id. When you're prompted for the password, answer with your email address.

4. Find the files you are looking for, using **cd** to change directories and **ls** to list the contents of the directory.

5. Set the mode of transfer to either ASCII or binary. The default is ASCII, so if you need to transfer a non-ASCII file, issue the **binary** command.

6. Transfer the files. Use **get** to copy the files to your local machine, or use **put** to transfer a file from your machine to the remote machine.

7. Disconnect from the remote machine with the **close** command.

8. Exit **ftp** with either **quit** or **bye**. They both do the same thing.

There are many more commands available for **ftp**, but these are the basic steps to get you started. Print out a copy of the **man** page for **ftp** before you start, keep it next to your terminal and you should have no problems. Most of the commands are either the same as or similar to their UNIX equivalents.

Using Telnet To Connect to a Remote Computer

The **telnet** command is similar to the **ftp** command in one important point. It's designed to work across a broad range of platforms, terminals and displays. And, like **ftp**, it has its good points and its bad points. If it's pretty and mouse-button-aware you want, **telnet** is not the tool. But if you have to connect to a remote computer with something that will almost always work, **telnet** will usually get the job done. To open a **telnet** session, use this syntax:

```
telnet [options] [hostname]
```

where the options include

  -a   Automatically login.

  -l *user* Send the user name if the remote system can accept it.

  -r   Use a similar interface to **rlogin**, with the escape character set to ~.

Other options are covered in the **man** pages, but these are the most common ones. Once connected to the remote machine, you can execute commands in a subshell with the **!** command, get help with the **?** command, or basically type in any command you would normally type in if you were remotely logged into that machine. In addition, there is a vast and hopelessly confusing set of options and toggles you can set inside **telnet**. These options let you configure and manipulate it so that it can handle almost any kind of system on the other end that allows you to connect in the first place. If you really need this kind of complexity, then nothing else will do. You'll just have to start with the **man** pages and an intimate knowledge of the quirks and foibles of the remote system and your system, and you should be able to get it all to work. But for most people, if you just treat **telnet** as if you had a simple, text-based login to the remote machine, you'll be fine.

Moving On

In this chapter we covered the shortcuts to making connections, starting with your work group and extending to the broader horizons of the Internet. This is one of the strengths of UNIX and part of the reason it continues to flourish as an operating system. In the next chapter, we cover an area we all hope to avoid—trouble.

10 Leading a Charmed Life

Anyone who has worked with computers for longer than a few minutes has, inevitably, done something they really wish they hadn't. And the longer you work with them, the more likely that something you do will cause you to feel a strong desire to rewind the clock and just undo the previous command or, worse, one you did a half-hour ago. Some operating systems are remarkably forgiving of one's inadvertent mistakes and allow you to undo all, or almost all, of whatever you just did.

Unfortunately, UNIX is not such an operating system. Unlike DOS, where programs like the Norton Utilities have given users tools to recover from disaster, there really aren't equivalents in the UNIX world. When you delete a file in UNIX it is pretty much gone forever. This changes the emphasis from disaster recovery to disaster avoidance, which is probably where it should be anyway.

The single biggest thing you can do to protect yourself in UNIX (or any other operating system, we might add) is to do regular backups. And how many times have you heard *that* one! Well, sorry, but you are going to get it again. We'll talk about specific backup strategies below, but right here we want to emphasize that there's no way to recover a deleted file other than by having a copy of it. So, either don't delete the file, or first be sure you have a backup copy of it you can recover.

But wait, you say. Your System Administrator does backups every day/week/whatever. Why should you have to worry about such things? After all, that's what a System Administrator gets paid the big bucks for, right? It's true. But even in the best of all possible worlds—where your system is completely backed up every night and there are never problems with the tape—this still isn't going to solve your problems.

First, do you really want to lose an entire day's worth of work? And even more to the point, restoring a single file from a system backup tape is *not* the sort of task that is likely to make your System Administrator happy. Yes, it can be done, and in the event of ultimate emergency this may be the only hope you have. But far better to take the necessary steps to protect yourself. In this chapter we examine two basic strategies for protection — risk avoidance and backup/recovery.

Risk Avoidance–Preventing Disaster

It's always easier not to make a mistake than to recover from it once the mistake is made. And wouldn't we all be better off if we ran our lives on that principle. So, how to avoid that mistake? Well, probably the first rule is to avoid certain irrevocable commands. UNIX makes it remarkably easy to simply remove entire directory structures without even a warning. Now, this power is impressive, if that is what you are sure you really want to do. But if that wasn't what you had in mind, then going "oops" won't help.

Trap **Don't use the rm -rf command.** This is one of those commands that is just too powerful for its own good. Actually, the ordinary **rm -r** command is really too powerful, but at least it will warn you before it starts deleting read-only files. When you add the **-f** (for force) switch, you have really left yourself no chance.

Tip 77 **Consider creating an alias for the rm command.** This is a touchy one. Some purists feel strongly that you shouldn't alias any of UNIX's built-in commands, while others do it all the time. We tend to think it's a bad practice if carried to the extreme, but in some cases it can be a lifesaver. For example, if you want to add an additional layer of protection, this is one way to do it. Try adding the following to your **.kshrc** file:

```
alias rm='rm -i'
```

Now, whenever you go to remove a file, you will be prompted for confirmation. The problem with this approach is that it can get pretty annoying if you have a bunch of files to remove, and you're really sure you want to remove them. Under those conditions, you can get careless about the removal, answering "y" to the prompt without really reading it. A better solution is to move the files out of the way temporarily, and only remove them when they are old enough that you are sure you want to get rid of them.

Tip 77 **Create an alias for rm that moves your files someplace safe.** This is the UNIX equivalent of some of the utilities available for DOS that move your files into a special holding directory. We have two simple little scripts we use. Both depend on your having a **tmp** directory under your $HOME directory, which is usually a good idea anyway. First, create the script **safe_rm.ksh** shown in Figure 10-1, and store it in your personal **bin** directory. Don't forget to make it executable with **chmod**. Now, create your alias for it:

```
alias rm='$HOME/bin/safe_rm.ksh'
```

and add that to your **.kshrc** file. To make this immediately available, resource your **.kshrc** file with this:

```
. ~/.kshrc
```

Now, every time you issue the **rm** command, what you are really doing is running the **safe_rm.ksh** script and moving the files to your **tmp** directory.

```
#!/bin/ksh
##############################################################################
#
# A script to move files to a temporary directory rather than remove them
# Use as an alias for the rm command.
#
if (mv $* ~/tmp)
then
    print "\nFiles have been moved to the ~/tmp directory. To remove them "
    print "use the purge command.\n\n "
else
    print "Error occurred, files not moved"
fi
~
~
~
~
~
~
~
~
~
~
"safe_rm.ksh" 14 lines, 384 characters
```

Figure 10-1: *A safer way to remove files.*

Tip

Purge your tmp directory of older files. If you're going to be stuffing all these files into your **tmp** directory, it will get crowded with junk over time. So you'll need to have a way to purge the older files and send them off to oblivion. Create a script to do this automatically, again with an alias. The script **purge.ksh**, shown in Figure 10-2, looks for all files in your **tmp** directory that haven't been changed in more than seven days, then asks if it's okay to delete them.

```
                                    XTerm
#!/bin/ksh
#################################################################
#
# A script to purge files which have been copied to the ~/tmp directory
# using the aliased rm command. Checks for files not changed in the last
# week, and removes them.
#
cd ~/tmp
if (find . -ctime +7 -ok rm {} \; )
then
    print "\nFiles older than 7 days in ~/tmp have been removed."
else
    print "Error occurred, files not removed"
fi
~
~
~
~
~
~
~
"purge.ksh" 15 lines, 429 characters
```

Figure 10-2: *A safe way to purge unneeded files in your* **tmp** *directory.*

Now, create an alias for this so you don't have to add that annoying **.ksh** to the end of the command each time.

```
alias purge='$HOME/bin/purge.ksh'
```

Notice that we were kind of conservative with this script. Even though it's only deleting the files that haven't been modified or changed in the last seven days, you'll still have to confirm each and every deletion. If you want a more forceful version, try the **purge!.ksh** shown in Figure 10-3.

```
┌──────────────────────────────────── XTerm ──────────────────────────────────┐
│ #!/bin/ksh                                                                    │
│ ###########################################################################  │
│ #                                                                            │
│ # A script to purge files which have been copied to the ~/tmp directory      │
│ # using the aliased rm command. Checks for files not changed in the last     │
│ # week, and removes them. This is the bang version. Also included in our     │
│ # crontab file to run once a week. Thus, all files in ~/tmp are absolutely   │
│ # removed after 14 days.                                                     │
│ #                                                                            │
│ cd ~/tmp                                                                     │
│ if (find . -ctime +7 -exec rm -f {} \: )                                     │
│ then                                                                         │
│     print "\nFiles older than 7 days in ~/tmp have been removed."            │
│ else                                                                         │
│     print "Error occurred, files not removed"                                │
│ fi                                                                           │
│                                                                              │
│ ~                                                                            │
│ ~                                                                            │
│ ~                                                                            │
│ ~                                                                            │
│ ~                                                                            │
│ ~                                                                            │
│ "purge!.ksh" 17 lines, 580 characters                                        │
└──────────────────────────────────────────────────────────────────────────────┘
```

Figure 10-3: The ***purge-bang*** script is for when you are really sure.

Of course, you will probably want to alias this one as well. So we have this alias:

```
alias purge!='$HOME/bin/purge!.ksh'
```

Now, anytime we want to clean up the directory of older files, and we're sure there's nothing in there we actually care about, we just use **purge!** to remove all the files at least seven days old from the **tmp** directory.

Tip

Add purge! to your crontab. We're not generally in favor of doing this sort of absolute cleanup automatically, but if you're a lazy sort or absolutely sure that files in your **tmp** directory are okay to delete, then you might consider adding this to your **crontab** if you have permission to use the **cron** process. One way to do this is to run it only every Sunday night. That way, you know that no file in the directory is more than two weeks old, but that nothing from last week has yet been removed. The crontab entry for this would be

```
0 1 * * 0 $HOME/bin/purge!.sh
```

Hmm, perhaps you notice a change? The name has gone from **purge!.ksh** to **purge!.sh,** and this is, of course, on purpose. When **cron** runs your **crontab** file, it only uses the basic Bourne shell to do so. Therefore, we modified the script accordingly, as shown in Figure 10-4.

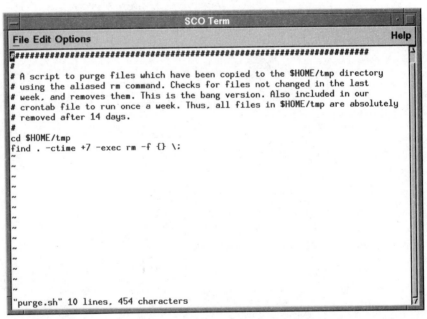

```
#################################################################
#
# A script to purge files which have been copied to the $HOME/tmp directory
# using the aliased rm command. Checks for files not changed in the last
# week, and removes them. This is the bang version. Also included in our
# crontab file to run once a week. Thus, all files in $HOME/tmp are absolutely
# removed after 14 days.
#
cd $HOME/tmp
find . -ctime +7 -exec rm -f {} \;
```

`"purge.sh" 10 lines, 454 characters`

Figure 10-4: *When you run a script from your **crontab** you have to use the Bourne shell.*

However, you don't want to leave yourself without a way to run the real **rm** command for those times when you really, really want to remove a file. So use yet another alias, this time to **rm!** in keeping with the convention we've been using.

```
alias rm!='/bin/rm'
```

This uses the absolute path to the **rm** command, which will get around any stray scripts someone may have out there, and go straight to the source.

Protection Strategies

One important way to protect your files from inadvertent removal or, even worse, deliberate mischief is to use the protection mechanisms built into UNIX.

Step one is to make really important files read-only. This is easy to do and can save you plenty of trouble. If you have files you don't need to change but do need to access regularly, change their permissions to not allow anyone, even yourself, to write to them.

```
chmod a-w filename
```

Now the file cannot be changed without taking extra steps, even by you the owner. Of course, you can get around this by changing the permissions before you change the file. But you have made the process awkward enough that you are unlikely to do it by accident.

Trap **The Superuser can delete your file no matter what you do.** This is one of those sad but true facts. No matter how much protection you put on a file, the Superuser can blithely delete the file, change it, or whatever, with barely a moment's thought—yet another reason to stay on friendly terms with this person.

Tip **Create a special script to edit read-only files.** If you want to make sure that some files are protected from casual change, it's quite easy to make a simple little script that modifies the permissions of the file, opens **vi** to edit it, and then changes the permissions back when you are done. We'll call it **vi!** for an alias:

```
alias vi!='$HOME/bin/vi!.ksh'
```

and we will use the script shown in Figure 10-5 for this.

```
#!/bin/ksh
############################################################################
#
# A script to edit files that are read only, and then return them to
# Read only status when you are done.
#
if (chmod u+w $* )
then
    vi $*
    chmod u-w $*
else
    print "Error occurred -- Unable to change permission to +w. "
fi
~
~
~
~
~
~
~
~
~
~
"vi!.ksh" 14 lines, 315 characters
```

Figure 10-5: *A simple script to edit read-only files.*

The nice part about this script is that it returns your permissions to their previous condition when you are done. This makes it relatively easy to edit a read-only file and yet maintain the protection from casual changes. This is usually a good compromise: somewhere between paranoia and carelessness.

Tip **Put sensitive or critical files in directories that are inaccessible to others.** Change the permissions on these directories using the **chmod** command to deny access to anyone except you and the Superuser.

```
chmod 700 dirname
```

This will make it impossible for anyone to accidentally or intentionally delete, change or even read the files in these directories. Unless someone has access to your password. Another good reason to keep your password safe.

Trap **Don't forget to change your $HOME directory as well.** Easy enough to protect your own directories, but one often forgets to change the home directory itself.

```
chmod 700 $HOME
```

will change just your home directory so that no one can come snooping around.

Backup, Backup, Backup!

All these nice tips for ways to protect against accidentally deleting files, or changing them when you don't mean to, are great. We strongly encourage you to use some combination of them. But nothing beats a *verified* backup when disaster strikes. The person with the primary responsibility for backups is the System Administrator, but everyone who works with computers needs to take responsibility for backups of their own critical files. This isn't hard, it need not be onerous, and it can be a lifesaver.

The beauty of UNIX is that you don't usually have to worry about backing up programs or huge data files, because these are generally the domain of the System Administrator. But you do need to think about your own, local data files. The method you use will vary depending on the capabilities of your system, the amount of hard-disk space available and exactly what programs and media are available to individual users on your system. But most systems have enough hard-disk space for you to maintain at least a copy of your most recent work on the hard disk. And if you have access and permissions, it's fairly easy to make copies of these files onto floppy disk. The key to making this painless is to only back up what you need to, and then do it *often*.

Personally, we prefer to do backups of current working files about twice a day, but you'll need to decide what works for you. Many users like to automate the process as part of their logout routine, and the C shell even has a special file for this purpose—**.logout**. But if you use the Korn shell, you'll need to create your own equivalent. But before we get into the particulars of how to automate backups, let's look at the kinds of backup you can, and should, do.

Hard Disk Backups

The modern hard disk is remarkably safe and stable, and it almost never crashes. Hard disks bought today have an average "Mean Time Between Failure" (MTBF) of 100,000 to 300,000 hours of continuous service, depending on the brand and model. That translates into anywhere from 11 to 34 *years* between failures. Which is certainly longer than you need to worry about, because computers bought today won't be in service in eleven years, much less 34 years. They'll be technologically obsolete long before. Of course, it's still possible to get a lemon, which is why the System Administrator faithfully does backups. So a backup to your hard disk may well be sufficient for your files. This will protect you against accidental erasure and the stray corruption of a critical file that may be caused by circumstances beyond your control.

Tip 77 Keep copies of your working files in a backup directory. This is probably the simplest way to handle your backup chores and will suffice for most users. We call ours **.backup** and have the permissions set to 700 (that's full permission for the owner but no permission whatsoever for anyone else). This should be enough to protect you from casual (or even not-so-casual) mischief, since the only other person who can get into this directory is the Superuser. Then, we keep current versions of our working files in that directory. For simple chores, where you don't need or want to keep different versions of your files, we have a simple alias we call whenever we are going to log out. It copies the files that have changed today into the **.backup** directory.

```
alias savwrk='find $HOME/* -mtime -1 -exec→
    cp {} $HOME/.backup \;'
```

This alias works pretty well, but it isn't perfect. It won't, for example, copy files or directories that start with a dot. The alternative is to add into this any special directories or files that you want to make sure are copied. Or write a script that builds a smarter directory tree.

Tape or Floppy Backups

Hard-disk backups are nice, and they are quite adequate protection for many purposes, especially considering that your System Administrator is undoubtedly doing periodic complete tape backups. But there are circumstances where they just aren't appropriate. If you are doing extremely sensitive work and can't leave copies of what you do on the hard disk, for example, you'll need to take the work off the hard disk when you aren't present. And if you would be totally devastated if you lost certain files, you probably want to do your own back-ups above and beyond what the System Administrator is doing. Especially if you are in an environment where the system-wide backups are done only weekly.

The most common mechanism for backing up files to an external storage medium such as tape or floppy is the UNIX **tar** (tape archive and restore) command. This command, which is available on virtually all UNIX systems and can be obtained for other systems such as DOS, is a simple and fairly efficient way to handle most backup chores that a user needs to do. The System Administrator may well have more powerful tools, which can easily span multiple machines and file systems on the network, but you aren't likely to need those, fortunately.

The syntax for the **tar** command is:

```
tar key files
```

where key is one of the following basic actions:

c   Create a new archive.

r   Append to an existing archive.

t   List the contents of the archive.

u   Update the archive, adding files that aren't present or are newer.

x   Extract the files from the archive.

Add one or more of the following modifiers:

A   Suppress absolute filenames.

l   Give an error message if a link can't be resolved.

L   Follow symbolic as well as hard links.

m   Don't restore modification times (everything gets current date/time).

p   Extract using the original permissions.

v   Verbose - normally **tar** is quiet.

w   Wait for confirmation before each action.

f   The next argument is the device name to use.

These are the most important of the tar options, and they behave pretty much consistently across a variety of platforms. There may well be specific options appropriate to your particular situation or implementation of **tar**, so check with your System Administrator if in doubt. The final argument for **tar** is the files to be archived. This can be specific files or directories, or **tar** can be part of a piped command line if the device is "-" for standard input or output.

Tip **Use tar to copy files to a different machine or file system.** Since **tar** follows subdirectories, it is easy to use for transferring complete directory structures to a different place. If, for example, you wanted to copy files to a new place, keeping everything intact, you could use

```
cd sourcedir;tar cf - . (cd targetdir;→
    tar xf -)
```

which would copy everything from the source directory to the target directory. It's important that you use the dot for the source directory here so that the archive is created with relative pathnames.

Tip **Use tar to back up your files to a floppy or tape drive.** If you have a floppy drive in your workstation, you probably already know what the device file name for it is. But if in doubt, ask your System Administrator and then write it down where you won't lose it. One possible place is right on the front of the floppy drive in permanent marker. A typical device might be **/dev/fd0** for the first floppy, so the **tar** command to save your entire home directory and all the files in it would be

```
tar cvf /dev/fd0 $HOME
```

If you want to save the files with relative path names, not the absolute ones that this would give you, change to your home directory first, then substitute a simple dot for the **$HOME** and you're in business.

Moving On

In this chapter we've explored some clever ways for protecting your files from disaster, both accidental mistakes as well as disasters caused by external forces which you can't control. In the next chapter, we're going to go into some of the more powerful aspects of the Korn shell. Here's where you'll have your chance to try some real legerdemain of your own.

11  The UNIX Treasure House

If you're ready to tackle some areas of UNIX that are a bit more advanced, this chapter will help you along. In it we'll explore more about the Korn shell and how to write shell scripts with it. We'll also learn a little bit about **awk**, a programming language available on most UNIX platforms for the manipulation of structured text into formatted reports, and an equally tiny bit about **perl**, a newer and in many ways more interesting programming language available in the public domain.

The Korn Shell

The Korn shell was invented by David Korn in the 1980's at AT&T's Bell Labs. It has gone through several iterations, but the one most commonly available was written in 1988 and has been distributed on a wide range of UNIX platforms since that time—especially those known as System V Release 4 (SVR4), though most flavors of UNIX based on the Berkeley System Distribution (BSD) also now support the Korn shell. The Korn shell continues to be developed, and new versions are likely to see the light of day over time.

Most of the examples we have used in this book have been written and tested under the Korn shell, and by this point in the book you've probably picked up quite a few little things about it. But we felt that it would be useful to give you a reference for some of the basics of shell programming, as opposed to interactive use, that the Korn shell supports—some that are less dense than the **man** pages.

Variables & Parameters

Like any programming tool, the Korn shell lets you define variables and accepts input parameters. Parameters are anything which appears on the command line (or is piped into the command) after the command itself. The Korn shell separates, or *parses,* these parameters by looking for white space in between them, or, more properly, whatever characters are in the IFS (internal field separator) variable. By default, this is space, tab, and newline. But you can change this to make it easier to parse a set of options. You should be sure, though, to set it back when you get done. The positional parameters are automatically assigned by the shell as **$1 $2 $3** and so forth. The value of **$0** is the name of the calling script. The variable **$*** holds all the values. Each value is separated by the first character of **IFS** as a single string, and the variable **$@** is equal to "$1" "$2", and so forth, as separate parameters.

You assign values to a variable with this syntax:

```
variable=value
```

So, for example,

```
wayne=harold
print "Wayne is now called $wayne"
```

results in

```
Wayne is now called harold
```

Korn Shell Math

You can do simple math within a Korn shell script, though if you want to do much of it, there are far better choices for programming languages than the Korn shell. But, for example, you can declare a variable, **i**, and assign a value to it:

```
i=100
let i=100
(( i=100 ))
```

All three of these statements will assign the value of 100 to the variable "i". To perform arithmetic in the Korn shell, you may use the operators in the following table:

Arithmetic Operators for the Korn Shell	
Operator	Action
+	Addition
-	Subtraction
*	Multiplication
/	Division (Truncates to integer value)
%	Modulus
<<	Bit shift left
>>	Bit shift right
&	Bitwise AND
|	Bitwise OR
~	Bitwise NOT
^	Bitwise XOR

Logical or Relational Operators in the Korn Shell

Operator	Action
<	Less than
>	Greater than
<=	Less than or equal to
>=	Greater than or equal to
!=	Not equal to
==	Equal to
&&	Logical AND
||	Logical OR

To tell the Korn Shell to evaluate an arithmetic expression, enclose it in double parentheses "(( ))". Even special characters lose their meaning inside these double parentheses, so you can use "*" without quoting or escaping it.

Trap **The Korn shell only does integer arithmetic.** You can use floating-point numbers, and it will accept them without an error message, but it truncates them so you may not get the answer you expect! For example, consider the following:

```
(( 7.2 / 1.8 ))
```

This should, you would expect, evaluate to 4. But the answer is actually 7 in the Korn shell, since it is really being evaluated as "7 div 1".

Even though the entire expression is enclosed in double parentheses, you still use additional parentheses inside the expression to control the order of precedence. So, for example, to multiply 7 times the result of adding 2+4 divided by 3, one would use:

```
(( 7 * ( (2+4)/3) ))
```

Note that the additional white space we've included in this line is not significant. We find, however, that it makes the line much easier to read.

String Operators

The Korn shell is much better at string operations than math operations, and when combined with the pattern-matching capabilities built into the Korn shell, you can do some pretty powerful text-manipulation without ever having to call on **awk** or **perl** or other text manipulation languages.

First, of course, is concatenation. To concatenate two strings in UNIX, simply stick them together, without intervening white space. If you need to include white space, enclosing the whole thing in quotes gets around the problem. This is shown in Figure 11-1, where we made up some examples for demonstration purposes.

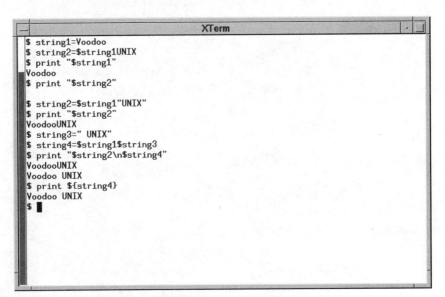

```
$ string1=Voodoo
$ string2=$string1UNIX
$ print "$string1"
Voodoo
$ print "$string2"

$ string2=$string1"UNIX"
$ print "$string2"
VoodooUNIX
$ string3=" UNIX"
$ string4=$string1$string3
$ print "$string2\n$string4"
VoodooUNIX
Voodoo UNIX
$ print ${string4}
Voodoo UNIX
$ 
```

Figure 11-1: *Concatenating strings in the Korn shell.*

The last line shown in Figure 11-1 actually leads us to the next topic. Most of the time, we refer to a string variable that we have created with a simple "$*strvar*" where the *strvar* is the variable. But this is actually a specific case of the more general syntax of "${*strvar*}" which works in all cases. So, for example, you can get away with referencing the ninth positional parameter you pass in to your script with a **$9** and all is well. But you can't get away with **$10**. To reference the tenth (and later) positional parameter, you need to be more formal by using the **${10}** syntax.

The Korn Shell also provides for quite useful string substitution operators. They let you check to see what the value of a string is, and then either substitute for the value, or use a default, or exit out of the script. The following table shows the possibilities.

The Korn Shell's Substitution Operators

Operator	Substitution
${*str:=expression*}	If *str* is unset or null returns *expression* and assigns *expression* to *str* as well. If *str* has a value, returns that value.
${*str:-expression*}	If *str* is unset or null returns *expression* but doesn't change *str*. If *str* has a value, returns that value.
${*str:+expression*}	If *str* is unset or null, returns null. If *str* has a value, it returns *expression*.
${*str:?expression*}	If *str* is unset or null, sends the value of *expression* to standard error, and aborts the current command or script. If *str* has a value, returns that value.
${*str#pattern*}	If *pattern* matches the beginning of *str* then it returns *str* with the smallest matching part deleted, otherwise it returns *str* unchanged.
${*str##pattern*}	If *pattern* matches the beginning of *str* then it returns *str* with the largest matching part deleted, otherwise it returns *str* unchanged.
${*str%pattern*}	If *pattern* matches the end of *str* then it returns *str* with the smallest matching part deleted, otherwise it returns *str* unchanged.
${*str%%pattern*}	If *pattern* matches the end of *str* then it returns *str* with the largest matching part deleted, otherwise it returns *str* unchanged.

You can use these operators to easily check if a variable has been set, and then do something depending on the answer to that test.

Trap You can't use the ${str:=expression} syntax to assign a value to a positional parameter. You'll have to use an intermediate local variable to get the job done. This is one nuisance in the Korn shell we have yet to see a good explanation or justification for.

Predefined Variables in the Korn Shell

There are a number of variables that are defined automatically by either the Korn shell or the **login** program, though you can redefine them if you want. We showed you how to do this in Chapter 4 when we redefined the PS1 variable to change our prompt. The following table shows the parameters and variables that are set by the Korn shell. The table after that shows the parameters and variables that are used by various aspects of the Korn shell.

Parameters Set by the Korn Shell

Parameter	Meaning or Use
#	The number of positional parameters currently set.
-	Flags passed to the shell on startup, or by the **set** command.
?	The value returned, in decimal, of the last command.
$	The process number of the current shell.
_	Initially the fully qualified pathname of the shell or script. Reassigned automatically to the last argument of the previous command.
!	The process number of the last background command.
ERRNO	The value of **errno** as set by the last failed system call.
LINENO	The current line number of the script being executed.
OLDPWD	The last working directory set by **cd**.
OPTARG	The last option returned by the **getopts** command.
OPTIND	The index (position) of the last option returned by the **getopts** command.
PPID	The process ID of the parent of the shell.
PWD	The current working directory.
RANDOM	A psuedo-random integer between 0 and 32767 that changes each time the parameter is referenced, using the previous value as a seed.
REPLY	Set by the **select** statement, or by **read** with no arguments.
SECONDS	The number of seconds since the shell was started.

Parameters Set by the Korn Shell

Parameter	Meaning or Use
CDPATH	Search path for the **cd** command.
COLUMNS	Number of columns in the current edit window.
EDITOR	Default editor to be used for command-line editing.
ENV	Pathname of the script to execute when a shell is invoked.
FCEDIT	Default editor for the **fc** command.
HISTFILE	Pathname of the command history file.
HISTSIZE	Number of commands to keep in the history file. Default value is 128.
HOME	The home directory. Default destination for **cd** command.
IFS	Internal Field Separators, normally **space**, **tab**, and **new-line**.
LINES	Number of lines in the current display window.
MAIL	Default mail file for the user.
MAILCHECK	How often to check to see if new mail has arrived in the $MAIL or $MAILPATH file. Default is 10 minutes (600 seconds).
MAILPATH	List of possible mail destinations, delimited by colons.
PATH	The command execution search path.
PS1	The primary command-line prompt (default is "$ ").
PS2	The secondary command-line prompt (default is "> ").
PS3	The prompt string used within a select loop (default is "#? ").
PS4	The execution trace prompt (default is "+ ").
SHELL	The pathname of the shell.
TMOUT	If set to >0, the time until the shell will automatically terminate if no command is entered at the PS1 prompt.
VISUAL	The default command line editor. Overrides EDITOR.

Flow Control

If one intends to get much accomplished with any programming language or environment, then one must have some form of flow control. The Korn Shell is no exception and it provides

* if/then/else
* for
* while
* until
* case
* select

This is an adequate selection of flow-control statements, but unfortunately the syntax is not exactly user-friendly. You'll probably find that it takes a certain amount of trial and error to get it all right.

If/Then/Else

This is the most basic and most commonly used form of flow control in a program. First you ask if something is true, and if it is you do something. If it isn't, you may do something else, or you may just do nothing. The basic syntax is

```
if condition
then
  statements
[elif condition2
  then statements]
[else
  statements]
fi
```

Each **if** is closed by a corresponding **fi** and within it can contain **else** and **elif** (else if) tests and statements. But the key to making the whole thing work is the *condition* part of the construct. And here the Korn shell gives us some power. The *condition* can be a simple test of the typical Boolean kind such as these:

```
if [[ $DISPLAY = "rci1:0.0" ]]
if (( n == 1 ))
if (( y >= 17 ))
```

or it can be the result of running a program or even a series of programs. In this case the result or return code of the final program will be evaluated for the condition. An example might be something like

```
if echo $PATH | grep X11
```

which will test true if the path includes "X11" anywhere in it. This could also be a "multiple choice test":

```
if ( echo $PATH | grep interbase ) ||→
    whence gdml
```

will test to see if the path contains "interbase" or if one of its programs, **gdml**, can be found. If either is true, then the condition will be true.

For Loops

The **for** construct lets you perform an operation a fixed number of times. This is useful when you need to perform an operation on a group of items, such as a list of file names. This is a bit different from the way a C or Pascal programmer might expect a **for** loop to behave. In that case, the syntax might be something like **for i:=1 to 10 do**. Here we're passing a list of items to a variable, changing the value of the variable each time the loop is run. The syntax for this construct is

```
for name [in list]
do
    statements that act on or use $name
done
```

Each time through the loop, the value of **$name** has a different value, as it goes through the items in **list,** one at a time.

While & Until Loops

The **while** loop combines a conditional test with a looping construct, and as long as the condition tests true, the loop will continue to run. Think about that for a moment. If you don't make absolutely sure that your **while** loop can eventually be false, you're never going to get out of it. The **until** loop is the exact opposite of a **while** loop. It will run until the condition is true. So the cardinal rule of **while** and **until** loops is to *first* make sure you define the exit condition. This will save you untold amounts of grief. The syntax for both is the same:

```
while condition
do
    statements
done
```

Just substitute **until** in the above if you want to test for a false condition instead of a true one.

Case Statements

The **case** statement is kind of like a multiple choice version of
the **if/then** clause. Its C counterpart is the **switch** statement.
But the Korn shell version lets you test a string against patterns
that can include wildcard characters and then, based on the
pattern it matches, perform a series of statements. This is really
nothing you can't do with a series of **if/then/elif** statements,
but it's expressed in a more concise way. The syntax is

```
case expression in
  pattern1)
    statements;;
  pattern2)
    statements;;

  ...
  patternN)
    statements;;
esac
```

Notice the double semicolons (;;) after each set of statements. These double semicolons must be used to finish each
leg of the case statement.

Because the case statement lets us match against a pattern,
it's especially useful for deciding what to do with a list of files.
We can easily feed the case statement a file list, one item at a
time, by enclosing the whole in a **for** loop and then, depending
on what kind of file it is, do something different with the file.
So, you could take output from a **find** command, for example,
that found every file that you hadn't changed in the last month
to create a file list, then do something with those files, depending on what sorts of files they were. You could remove all of
them with "tmp" in the name, move any with "sav" in the
name to an archive directory, and so forth. Figure 11-2 shows
a script to do just that.

```
                              SCO Term
 File Edit Options                                          Help
$ cat clean
#!/bin/ksh
# File: clean
# Check for old files and clean up after yourself
#
for file in $(find $HOME -ctime +30 -print)
do
        case $file in
                *tmp)
                        rm -i $file;;
                *sav*)
                        mv $file $HOME/archive;;
                core)
                        rm $file;;
        esac
done

$ █
```

Figure 11-2: *Case lets you do different things with different files, all in one easy-to-understand statement.*

The Select Statement

The Korn shell's **select** construct is a unique way to build a simple menu and branch based on the response to that menu. The **select** statement doesn't really line up with any corresponding statement in C or Pascal or any other language we know about. But it makes it easy for you to do things that might otherwise be a nuisance. The basic syntax of select is

```
select var [in list]
do
  statements that act on or use $var
done
```

This looks a lot like the syntax of a **for** loop—and it should, because they are, in fact, the same. The difference is that with the select construct we don't pass everything in the *list* to the do...done part, but only what the user selects from the menu that's displayed. Figure 11-3 shows how this works.

```
$ cat pets
PS3='favorite pet? '
select var in Cats Dogs Birds Fish
do
        case $var in
                Cats)
                        print "Cats are my favorite pet";;
                Dogs)
                        print "Dogs make friendly pets";;
                Birds)
                        print "Birds are a cheerful addition to the house";;
                Fish)
                        print "Fish make for a quiet pet";;
        esac
        break
done
$ pets
1) Cats
2) Dogs
3) Birds
4) Fish
favorite pet? 1
Cats are my favorite pet
$
```

Figure 11-3: *The Korn shell's* **select** *builds simple menus automatically.*

This should give you a feel for the different ways the Korn shell lets you control the flow of your script. The choice of which construct to use will depend on the circumstances, needs and often just the personal preferences of the person writing the script. The Korn shell's scripting abilities are probably enough for most users. But if you find they don't quite get the job done for a specific task you have in mind, we suggest you consider two extremely powerful alternatives that are either already in the UNIX you have or can be obtained fairly easily. Virtually all versions of UNIX include **awk**, and you (or your System Administrator) can easily obtain a version of **perl** if one isn't already on your system. Both provide the ability to do things that just can't be done, or at least not without considerable effort, in any of the available UNIX shells. Of course you can always become a C programmer—a thought that's bound to make **awk** more attractive.

The awk Programming Language

Awk is named for its three codevelopers, Alfred Aho, Peter Weinberger and Brian Kernighan. It's a pattern-matching language that can be used for simple tasks or for complex text manipulations. It's available as part of the standard UNIX distribution in its original form, at least, and usually also in a later version called "**new awk**," or **nawk**, written in 1985 by the original authors. If you get serious about **awk**, you'll want to make sure your system has the **nawk** version. Or you can obtain the GNU version, **gawk**, which adds most of the same enhancements to the original that **nawk** did. We'll use **awk** for this discussion.

The **awk** program is called with this command-line syntax:

```
awk [option] [script] [file]
```

The most common option is **-f** *scriptfile,* which reads in the script from a file instead of on the command line. An **awk** program consists of this form:

```
pattern {action}
```

where either the pattern-matching part or the action part is optional. If no pattern is specified, then action is performed on every line of the input. If no action is specified, then the default action of { print $0 } is performed on each line that matches the pattern. Since "$0" is a special parameter whose value is the entire line of input, the result is that the default action is to print the line that matches the input. This leads to one obvious use of **awk** as a somewhat more sophisticated version of **grep**. For example, the following will look for every line in a file that begins with a number and then print out the entire line.

```
awk '/^[0-9]/ ' filename
```

Obviously there are more powerful uses for **awk** than as a simple replacement for **grep**, but this does help point out a bit about the syntax of **awk**. Here we've used **awk** simply as a command-line program. The program we want to run is enclosed in single quotes to make sure that the shell doesn't try to interpret it. And we've used the same regular expression syntax we are accustomed to—except that the pattern is delimited by slashes ("/"). The pattern we're trying to match is the start of the line (the ^ part), followed immediately by a digit (the [0-9] part).

But how about a slightly more useful example? Suppose you want to count the number of lines in a file. You could use **wc** to do this, of course, but how are you going to find out anything about **awk** by using **wc**? Figure 11-4 shows two versions of the linecount script, as well as the results of running them, and the results of running the **wc** program to count the lines.

```
$ cat linecount.awk
# awk script to count lines in a file
END    {
              print "The file \""FILENAME"\" has", lc, "lines. "
       }
{ ++lc }
$ awk -f linecount.awk safe_rm.ksh
The file "safe_rm.ksh" has 14 lines.
$ cat linecount
#!/usr/bin/awk -f
# awk script to count lines in a file
END    {
              print "The file \""FILENAME"\" has", lc, "lines. "
       }
{ ++lc }
$ linecount safe_rm.ksh
The file "safe_rm.ksh" has 14 lines.
$ wc -l safe_rm.ksh
      14 safe_rm.ksh
$ ▉
```

Figure 11-4: *Three different ways to count the lines in a file.*

The first version is intended to be run by an explicit call to
awk with this as the script file for **awk** to use. It has a single
header comment line to keep it very small so it will all fit on
the screen. But you would, of course, add additional information in your initial header. Then it has the reserved word
"END" followed by an action enclosed in braces to print the
message with the number of lines in the file. The word END
tells **awk** to only do this once, after all other processing has
been completed. There is an equivalent reserved word, "BE-
GIN," which lets you do a set of actions before you start
processing the file.

Also notice the word "FILENAME" in the middle of that
print statement. This is another reserved word that contains
the file name of the file being processed. If the script is processing standard input, the variable will return "-". Included in this
print statement is the variable "lc" which is one we made up
and that we didn't have to initialize, declare or do any of that
other boring programming stuff to.

Finally, we have the actual counting. Here, we have the very C-like expression "++lc"—a shorthand way of writing out the more verbose "lc = lc + 1" — which would be equally accept-able to **awk**. Notice that we didn't have to initialize **lc** to anything; it simply starts out life with a value of zero unless we give it some other. Since we want to start counting from one, not zero, we use the C construct of "++lc" which says to increment **lc** before we evaluate it, keeping us one ahead.

The second version of the line-counting program is what we like to think of as the stand-alone version. It uses the Korn shell's ability to execute a program directly by inserting that line that looks like a comment as the first line in the file. This line tells the Korn shell to process the rest of the file through the **awk** program using the **-f** option which will feed it the rest of the file as an **awk** script. This is the minimalist version of what is known as a "shell wrapper." It provides a handy way to run your favorite scripts without having to type in that more awkward command-line syntax.

You can do far more sophisticated wrappers to parse for command-line options, and so forth, but this is good enough for our purposes. Now we just type in **linecount** *filename* and we can count the number of lines in the file.

Finally, a more interesting version of the program. Figure 11-5 shows how this would look if we modified it to count only the comment lines in the file.

```
                          XTerm
$ cat comcnt
#!/usr/bin/awk -f
# awk script to count lines in a file
END    {
          print "The file \""FILENAME"\" has", cc, "comment lines. "
       }
/^#/ && !/^#!/ { ++cc }
$ comcnt safe_rm.ksh
The file "safe_rm.ksh" has 5 comment lines.
$ ▌
```

Figure 11-5: *Using **awk** to count the number of comments in a file.*

Here we used the same basic program. But now we told
awk to count the lines only if they began with a leading "#".
We even told it to ignore that initial line that we use on some
of our scripts to make sure they're processed using a particular
program or shell.

This is only the tiniest beginning of the ways you can use
awk to handle tasks in your day-to-day life. You can combine
the powerful pattern-matching abilities with the ability to act
on only that part of the input that matches the pattern to
create useful, easy-to-read formatted reports and documents.
(See Appendix C for sources of information about **awk**.) Next
we'll look at the newcomer to the formatting wars, **perl**.

The Perl Programming Language

Unlike **awk**, which was written by three people, **perl** was written essentially by a single person, Larry Wall. Others inevitably have influenced its growth and nature, but ultimately the blame rests with Larry. As does the credit, of course. **Perl** is officially short for "Practical Extraction and Report Language," which is a good enough description as far as it goes. But consider that a widely accepted view is that it's in fact short for "Pathologically Eclectic Rubbish Lister," and you'll begin to get a more accurate feel for the character of both the language and its creator. Most people who've tried **perl** seem to either adopt it for a wide variety of uses, or run screaming into the night. Whether **awk** or **perl** is a good choice for you, you'll have to decide on your own. But we do think that you should add one or the other to your everyday toolbox. We tend to think that the greater flexibility and power of the expanded regular expressions in **perl** give it a slight edge. Besides, as eclectic as its syntax is, it tends to grow on you.

In this section we'll take the two scripts that we created for **awk** and "port" them to **perl**. The end results are the same of course, but you'll be able to see some of the differences between **awk** and **perl**.

We'll bypass the command-line version of the line-counting program and go straight to the version with the minimalist shell wrapper around it. Except now instead of running the **awk** program, this will run the **perl** program. Normally, you would have the line

```
#!/usr/bin/perl
```

as the first line of your **perl** scripts. But ours is in an unusual place, so our first line reads

```
#!/work/bin/perl
```

The results are the same, however. This line tells the shell program that its sole job is to execute the **perl** program and just pass the statements in the file directly to **perl** to deal with. Figure 11-6 shows the two **perl** scripts for counting the number of lines in a file, and the number of comment lines in a file, the same two tasks we did with **awk**. But now the programs look a bit different.

```
XTerm
$ cat lc.p
#!/work/bin/perl
# perl script to count lines in a file
$filename =  $ARGV[0];
while (<>) {
    ++$lc
    }
print ("The file \"$filename\" has $lc lines.\n ");
$ cat comcnt.p
#!/work/bin/perl
# perl script to count comment lines in a file
$filename =  $ARGV[0];
while (<>) {
    if (/^#/ && !/^#!/) {
        ++$lc;
    }
}
print ("The file \"$filename\" has $lc comment lines.\n ");
$ 
```

Figure 11-6: *Our two scripts, re-written for Perl.*

Awk uses an implicit **while** loop that automatically sends the entire contents of the files given on the command line to the pattern-matching and action part of the program. But in the **perl** example, you see that we need to build the **while** loop explicitly, with this statement:

```
while (<>) {
  ++$lc;
}
```

That probably makes sense to you because most programming languages expect you to create your own **while** loops where you need them. But what's that "(<>)" supposed to mean. Well, that is known as the "diamond operator." It takes the file in the array $ARGV[0], which was the file we passed to the program on the command line, and examines each line of that program until it reaches the end. This is what the **awk** script did automatically.

The other thing that the **awk** program did automatically that we have to do explicitly here is pass in the file name we're counting the lines of. Here we need to stick that file name into a variable that won't get mucked up during the **while** loop so we can reference it at the end after we've counted all the lines.

In the second program, to count the comment lines in the file, we see again the differences and similarities between the two languages. In **awk** we simply added the pattern-matching criteria to the beginning of the line that did the counting. But here we need to add an explicit **if** clause. Again, some things that **awk** does automatically have to be explicitly called out in **perl**. We don't find this a hardship; in fact, we even think it makes the resultant code a bit easier to read. But others feel strongly that this is not as elegant.

It's important to notice the identical code describing the pattern match. While **perl** does add important new pattern-matching tools (our favorite is "\b" to define a word boundary), it still uses the same syntax as **awk**.

As you can see, there are substantial differences between **perl** and **awk**, even though both perform many of the same functions. In the broader sense, **perl** goes beyond where **awk** is or is likely to go, and is continuing to be actively developed. It is not, however, a part of the normal UNIX distribution, though it is freely available.

To Summarize

In this chapter we've touched on some more details about the Korn shell and how to use it to write shell scripts that can help automate your UNIX tasks. We also took a brief look at two text-manipulation and reporting languages, **awk** and **perl**, that can enhance your UNIX recipe book of magical incantations. Both are powerful, flexible tools that can help you manipulate data into a format that makes it easier to understand and more effective. Finally, the Glossary in the back of the book can help to make clear some of the more baffling UNIX-speak. Appendices A, B and C include a command reference, some translations of the more cryptic UNIX error messages and a source guide to help you take the tips you have learned in this book on to the next stage in your UNIX journey. We hope it is a fruitful and even a fun one for you.

Section II

UNIX
RESOURCES

Command Reference

Of course, you know that there are hundreds of commands in the various versions of UNIX, so don't be surprised that you don't find all of them here. You *will* find a lot of very useful ones—especially the ones used for the tricks in this book. We'll show you the syntax, the available options and a little on how each command works.

Because there are variations among the flavors of UNIX, your version may have a few more (or slightly different) options than the ones shown here. If you see a command that looks like it might do what you want to do and yet you don't see exactly the right option, check your documentation for possible variations.

COMMAND: **alias** *[options] name[='cmd']*

Objective: Assigns a shorthand name to substitute for *cmd*. If *='cmd'* is omitted, it prints the alias for *name*. Korn shell only.

Options & Variables

-t Creates a tracked alias for a UNIX command. The shell will remember the full pathname of the command, making it easier to find.

-x Exports the alias so it can be used in shell scripts.

COMMAND: **at** *options time [date] [+increment]*

Objective: Lets you schedule jobs to be executed later.

Options & Variables

-l *[jobID]*　　　　　Lists your currently scheduled jobs. Include a **jobID** if you want information on just one job.

-r *[jobID]*　　　　　Removes specified job from the queue. You can remove only your own jobs unless you're the Superuser.

time　　　　　Specifies the time the job should start. The format is *hh:mm [modifiers]*. A 24-hour clock is assumed unless you add the modifier **am** or **pm**, then time is based on a 23-hour clock.

COMMAND: **bg** *[jobIDs]*

Objective: Put current job or specified **jobIDs** in the background. Korn shell only.

COMMAND: **cal** *month year*

Objective: Displays a calendar on the standard output.

Options & Variables

month　　　　　Use a number between 1 and 12 or enough letters to represent a unique month.

year　　　　　Any number between 1 and 9999. You have to include all four digits.

COMMAND: **cancel** *requestIDs* or **cancel** *printer*

Objective: Cancels a print request generated by the **lp** spooler.

Options & Variables

requestIDs	Cancels by *requestID* number. Use **lpstat** to see a list of *requestIDs*.
printer	Cancels the current print job for this printer.

COMMAND: **cat** *[options] filelist*

Objective: Concatenates (joins) files together. Use the > operator to combine several files into a new file or use >> to append files to an existing file.

Options & Variables

-e	Print a $ to mark the end of each line. This option valid with the -v option.
-v	Displays control characters and other nonprinting characters.
-s	Suppresses messages about unreadable files.
-t	Print each tab as ^I and each form feed as ^L.
-u	Prints output as unbuffered.
filelist	Optional list of files to be joined.

COMMAND: **cd** *directoryname*

> **Objective:** Changes the current working directory.
>
> **Options & Variables**
>
> | | |
> |---|---|
> | *directoryname* | The name of the directory you want to make current. |

COMMAND: **chmod** *mode files*

> **Objective:** Changes the mode of files. A file's mode controls the permissions for access associated with that file. Only the owner of a file (or the Superuser) can change its mode.
>
> **Who**
>
> | | |
> |---|---|
> | u | User |
> | g | Group |
> | o | Others |
> | a | All (default) |
>
> **Opcode**
>
> | | |
> |---|---|
> | + | Add permission. |
> | - | Remove permission. |
> | = | Set permission to be only what's specified. |

Permission

r	Read
w	Write
x	Execute
s	Set user (or group) ID.

COMMAND: **cp** *[options] file1 file2*

Objective: Copies files.

Options & Variables

file1	The file to copy
file2	The destination name

COMMAND: **date** *MMDDhhmmyy or date +format*

Objective: Displays the system date and time.

Options & Variables
MMDDhhmmYY

MM	The month (01-12)
DD	The day (01-31)
hh	The hour (00-23)
mm	The minute (00-59)
YY	The year (00-99) —optional

Options & Variables

+format Consists of a % followed by:

n	Inserts a newline.
t	Inserts a tab.
m	Month (digits)
d	Day of month (digits)
y	Last two digits of year
D	Date as mm/dd/yy
i	Hour
M	Minute
S	Second
W	Day of week (0-6, 0=Sunday)

COMMAND: **diff** *[options] oldfile newfile*

Objective: Compares two text files to find where they differ.

Options & Variables

-b	Ignore repeating blanks and end-of-line blanks.
-e	Generate a script for the editor **ed**.
-f	Produce a script to recreate *file1* from *file2*.

COMMAND: **echo** *-n string*

> **Objective:** Writes the string to standard output. By default, **echo** follows all output with a newline. *-n* suppresses this. The special escape characters preceded by \ will produce special output sequences:

> **Character Meaning**

\b	Backspace
\c	Don't print a newline at the end (same as *-n*).
\f	Form feed
\n	Newline
\r	Carriage return
\t	Tab character
\\	Backslash

COMMAND: **fg** *[jobIDs]*

> **Objective:** Put current job or specified **jobIDs** in the foreground.

<u>COMMAND:</u> **find** *pathname condition*

Objective: Searches the specified directories, generating a list of files that match the criteria specified.

Options & Variables

-name *file*	Matches the specified *file*. If enclosed in quotation marks (" "), *file* can contain wildcards (*) and question marks (?).
-perm *mode*	Matches all files whose mode matched the numeric value of *mode*. All modes must be matched—not just read, write and execute. To match everything except this mode use, *-mode*.
-type *x*	Matches all files whose type is *x*, in which *x* is the following:

    c   Character device

    b   Block special

    d   Directory

    p   Named pipe

    f   Regular file (none of the preceding types)

-atime *days*	Matches all files last accessed *days* ago.
-mtime *days*	Matches all files last modified *days* ago.
-newer *file*	Matches all files modified more recently than *file*.

-ctime +*n* | -*n* | *n*	Matches files that were changed more than *n* (+*n*), less than *n* (-*n*) or exactly *n* (*n*) days ago. Change refers to modification, permission or ownership changes.
-exec *command*	Run the UNIX *command* on each file matched by **find**.
-ok *command*	Same as -exec but prompts for confirmation before the command is executed.
-print	Prints the names of the files found
-user	Matches files belonging to a *user* name or ID.

COMMAND: **finger** *[options] users*

Objective: Displays information about users on the system.

Options & Variables

-b	Omit user's home directory and shell from the output.
-f	Suppresses header lines.
-l	Forces the long output.
-p	Doesn't print the **.plan** file.
-q	Displays a quick list of users.
-s	Displays a short format.
users	Specify either an exact **login** name or as a first or last name.

COMMAND: **grep** *[options] regexp [files]*

Objective: Searches for a pattern or regular expression [*regexp*] in files and reports when it finds it.

Options & Variables

-c	Prints only a count of matched lines.
-l	Displays only the names of files containing a match.
-i	Eliminates case sensitivity.
-v	Prints all lines that *don't* match.
-n	Prints matching lines and line numbers.
-s	Suppresses error messages for nonexistent or unreadable files.

COMMAND: **head** *[-lines files]*

Objective: Prints the first few lines of a file.

Options & Variables

-lines	Specifies the number of lines to print. The default is 10.
files	A list, separated by spaces, of the files you want printed. The default is standard input.

COMMAND: **jobs** *[options] [jobIDs]*

Objective: Lists running or stopped jobs. Include *jobIDs* to check on specific jobs. Korn shell only.

Options & Variables

-l	List job IDs and process group IDs.
-n	List only the jobs with status changes since the last notification.
-p	List process group IDs only.

COMMAND: **lp** *[options] [files]*

Objective: Sends *files* to the printer.

Options & Variables

-c	Copies *files* to print spooler.
-d *dest*	Sends output to printer named *dest*.
-f *form-name* [-d any]	Spooler prints the request only when the specified *form-name* is mounted on the printer. With the **-d any** option set, the request goes to any printer with *form-name* mounted.
-L	Sends the print job to the printer attached to the terminal.
-n *number*	Specifies the *number* of copies to print.
-P *pages*	Prints on the page numbers specified in *pages*.

-R	Removes file after printing.
-t *title*	Use *title* on the printout's banner page.

COMMAND: **lprint** - *file*

Objective: Sends a *file* to a printer attached to the terminal.

Options & Variables

-	Print from standard input instead of *file*.

COMMAND: **lpstat** *[options]*

Objective: Shows the status of the lp spooler system and print requests.

Options & Variables

-a *list*	Shows whether the printers in *list* are accepting requests.
-c *list*	Shows the class names of the printers in *list*.
-p *list*	Shows the status of the printers in *list*. Usually used to make sure a printer is enabled.
-d	Shows the default printer destination.
-f *list*	Verifies that the *list* of forms is known to **lp**.
-r	Shows whether the print scheduler is on or off.

| -s | Shows a status summary (almost everything). |
| -t | Shows all status information (reports everything). |

COMMAND: ls *[options] [directories]*

Objective: Lists contents of directories. If no *directories* are given, lists the files in the current directory.

Options & Variables

-A	Shows all files, including hidden files (files that start with a period). Doesn't include the current directory or parent directory.
-a	Shows all files including the current directory (.) and the parent directory (..).
-C	Lists files in columns.
-x	Lists files in rows going across the screen.
-d	Lists only directory names, not their contents.
-l	Gives a long listing including permissions, owner, size, file name, date last modified and so forth.

COMMAND: **mail** *[options]* *[usernames]*

Objective: Read mail or send mail to other users. You can type ? for a summary of commands.

Options & Variables

-e	Checks for mail in your incoming mailbox.
-f *file*	Opens *file* to read mail. If no *file* is specified, the mbox file is used.
-F	Stores outgoing mail in a file with the same name as that of the first recipient of the message.
-H	Shows a header summary of the mailbox contents.
-s *subject*	Sets the subject line in the mail header to *subject*.
-u	Reads user's incoming mailbox.

COMMAND: **make** *[options]* *[targets]* *[macro definitions]*

Objective: Updates one or more targets according to dependency instructions in a description file in the current directory. This file is called **makefile** or **Makefile** by default. Options, targets and macro definitions can appear in any order. Macro definitions are typed as *name=string*.

Options & Variables

-e	Overrides **makefile** assignments with environment variables.
-f *makefile*	Use *makefile* as the description file.
-i	Ignores command error codes.
-n	Prints commands but doesn't execute.
-p	Prints macro definitions and target description.
-q	Query. Returns 0 if the file is up to date, nonzero otherwise.
-r	Don't use default rules.
-s	Don't display command lines.
-t	Touch the target files. Causes them to be updated.

COMMAND: **man/usr/bin/man** *[options] [section] [title]*

Objective: Displays information from the online reference manuals.

Options & Variables

-a	Shows all pages matching *title*.
-b	Leave blank lines in output
-d*dir*	Specifies the directory *dir* to be added to the search path for entries.

COMMAND: **mesg** *n y*

> **Objective:** Controls whether or not others can send messages to your screen.
>
> **Options & Variables**
>
> | | |
> |---|---|
> | n | Doesn't let users send messages to your terminal. |
> | y | Allows messages (the default). |

COMMAND: **mkdir** *[options] dirname*

> **Objective:** Makes new directories.
>
> **Options & Variables**
>
> | | |
> |---|---|
> | -m *mode* | Sets the access *mode* for all new directories. |
> | -p | Creates all intervening parent directories if they don't already exist. |
> | *dirname* | The name of the new directory. |

COMMAND: **more** *[options] [files]*

> **Objective:** Displays the named files on screen at a time. Press return to get the next line or press the spacebar to get the next screen.

Options & Variables

-c	Page through the file by clearing each window instead of scrolling. This is sometimes faster.
-f	Counts logical lines instead of screen lines.
-l	Ignore form feed characters (^L).
-r	Force display of control characters in the form ^x.
-s	Display multiple blank lines as one.

COMMAND: **mv** *[option] source target*

Objective: Moves or renames files or directories.

Options & Variables

-f	Overwrites existing files, regardless of permissions settings.

Source	Target	Result
File	*name*	*Rename file as* name.
File	Existing File	Overwrite existing file.
Directory	*name*	Rename directory as *name*.
Directory	Existing directory	Make directory a subdirectory of existing directory.
File(s)	Existing directory	Move files to directory.

COMMAND: **newgrp** *group*

Objective: Changes a user's group identification. Only the group ID is changed, the user remains a member of all groups previously assigned. If you omit the *group* name, you're returned to the group you're in at login.

COMMAND: **news** *[options] [items]*

Objective: Reads news posted in the **/usr/news** directory. With no arguments, **news** prints all current items. This is not an interface for USENET news.

Options & Variables

-a	Shows all news items, whether current or not.
-n	Lists names of articles, not their contents.
-s	Reports the number of current items.

COMMAND: **nice** *[option] command*

Objective: Execute a command with lower priority. In other words, make nice with the other users.

Options & Variables

-n	Run the *command* with a niceness level of *n* (1-19). The default is 10. The higher the *n*, the nicer you're being.

COMMAND: **openwin** *[options]*

Objective: Sets up OpenWindows, the windowing environment based on the Open Look graphical user interface.

Options & Variables

-banner   Displays the OpenWindows banner screen at startup.

-noauth   Reverts to a lower security mode.

-includedemo   Includes the path to the demo directory in the user's search path.

COMMAND: **pack** *[option] files*

Objective: Compresses files so they take up less space.

Options & Variables

-                    Print more statistical information such as the number of times each byte is used, relative frequency and so forth.

files   A space-delimited list of the files to be packed.

COMMAND: **passwd** *[options]*

Objective: Lets you change your own password.

Options & Variables

-s   Displays password information such as user name, password status, date last changed, and so forth.

COMMAND: **pg** *[options] files*

> **Objective:** Lets you view text files one page at a time. Unlike **more**, lets you move backward as well as forward. Pressing ^ while in pg places you in reverse search mode. Pressing / returns you to forward search mode.

> **Options & Variables**

> | | |
> |---|---|
> | -e | No pause at the end of a file. |
> | -f | Don't split long lines. |
> | -n | Issues a **pg** command without waiting for a carriage return. |
> | -s | Messages and prompts display in standout mode (reverse video). |
> | *+number* | Begin display at line *number*. |
> | *+/pattern* | Start display at the first line containing *pattern*. |
> | *files* | A list of space-delimited file names. |

COMMAND: **ping** *[options] host*

> **Objective:** Tells you if another machine on the network is operational. This command sends out an ECHO_REQUEST packet to the specified machine. If the packet is sent and received successfully, the connection is considered alive.

Options & Variables

-n   Displays network addresses as
                      numbers.

-c *count*   Stop after sending *count*
                      ECHO_RESPONSE packets.

-r   Bypass the normal routing tables and
                      send directly to a *host* on an attached
                      network.

COMMAND: **pr** *[options] files*

Objective: Lets you format a file while printing it to the standard output.

Options & Variables

+*page*   Begins printing at the page number
                      page.

-*col*   Specifies *col* columns of output.

-a   Prints files in a multicolumn format.

-d   Double-spaces the output.

-f   Separates the pages with a single form
                      feed command.

-m   Merges the files, printing each file in a
                      column. Overrides the -*col* option.

-t   Doesn't print the header or footer.

COMMAND: **purge** *[options] files*

Objective: Gets rid of files by overwriting them. These can be files on the command line or files listed in a special policy file maintained by the System Administrator.

Options & Variables

-f	Don't warn about files that don't exist or are inaccessible.
-m *number*	Overwrites each file *number* times.
-r	Recursively purges directories.
-s	Overwrites files in the policy file that are designated as system files.
-u	Overwrites files in the policy file that are designated as user files.
-t *group*	Overwrites files in the policy file that are designated as the type *group*.
-v	Lists the name of each file as it's overwritten.
files	A space-delimited list of files to purge. May be regular files, directories or special-character files.

COMMAND: **pwd**

Objective: Prints the full path name of the current working directory.

<u>COMMAND:</u> **rcp** *[options] hostname:file1 hostname:file2*

Objective: Copies files between two machines.

Options & Variables

-p   Preserves modification times and modes of the original files.

-r   If the source and target are both directories, copies each subtree rooted at that name.

<u>COMMAND:</u> **rlogin** *[options] system*

Objective: Lets you log in to a remote computer.

Options & Variables

-8   Allows 8-bit-data transfers instead of 7-bit-data.

-e*c*   Specifies the escape character c.

-l *username*   Logs into the remote system using *username*. The default is the same as your local username.

COMMAND: **rm** *files*

> **Objective:** Removes one or more files. To remove a file, you must have write permission for the directory that contains the file. If you don't have write permission for the file itself, you'll be prompted to confirm the deletion. This can be a very dangerous command. **Be careful.**
>
> **Options & Variables**
>
> | | |
> |---|---|
> | -f | Remove write-protected files without prompting. |
> | -i | Prompts for each deletion. |
> | -r | If *files* is a directory, remove the entire directory and its contents. |

COMMAND: **rmdir** *[options] directoryname*

> **Objective:** Removes directories. The directory has to be empty first.
>
> **Options & Variables**
>
> | | |
> |---|---|
> | -p | Removes *directoryname* and any intervening parent directories that become empty as a result. |
> | -s | Suppresses standard error messages that result from using -p. |

COMMAND: **sdiff** *[options] file1 file2*

Objective: Produce a side-by-side comparison of *file1* with *file2*.

Output is

text text	Identical lines.
text <	Line exists only in *file1*.
> text	Line exists only in *file2*.
text|text	Lines are different.

Options & Variables

-w*width*	Specifies that the output line is to be *width* characters.
-l	Identical lines appear only on the left side of the output.
-s	Doesn't show identical lines.
file1	File in the left column of the output.
file2	File in the right column of the output.

COMMAND: **set**

Objective: Displays the values of all shell variables.

COMMAND: **setcolor** *[options] [argument]*

> **Objective:** Set screen color and other attributes.
>
> **Options & Variables**
>
> | | |
> |---|---|
> | -b *color* | Set background color to *color*. |
> | -g *color1 color2* | Sets foreground to *color1* and background to *color2*. |
> | -n | Sets the screen to "normal," a white foreground and a black background. |
> | -r *color1 color2* | Sets the screen's reverse-video foreground to *color1* and the screen's reverse-video background to *color2*. |
> | -o *color* | Sets the border to *color*. |

COMMAND: **sleep** *seconds*

> **Objective:** Suspends execution of a process for the number of *seconds* specified.

COMMAND: **sort** *[options] [files]*

> **Objective:** Sorts the lines of the named *files*.
>
> **Options & Variables**
>
> | | |
> |---|---|
> | -b | Ignores leading spaces and tabs. |
> | -c | Checks to see if the files are already sorted and if they are, produces no output. |

-d	Sorts in dictionary order.
-f	Ignores uppercase and lowercase differences.
-i	Ignores nonprintable characters.
-m	Merges sorted input files.
-n	Sorts by numeric order.
-r	Reverses the order of the sort.
-u	Identical lines in the input appear only once in the output.

COMMAND: **spell** *[options]* *+userdict files*

Objective: Checks the spelling of a text file.

Options & Variables

-b	Uses British spelling.
-v	Displays all words not literally in the dictionary.
-x	Shows every possible word stem.
+userdict	Use the sorted *userdict* as a local dictionary to add to the system dictionary.

COMMAND: **strings** *[options] files*

> **Objective:** Searches for ASCII characters in binary files.
>
> **Options & Variables**
>
> | | |
> |---|---|
> | - | Search the entire file, not just the initialized data portion of object files. |
> | -o | Shows the byte offset in the file where the string was found. |
> | - *number* | Minimum string length is *number*. Default is 4. |

COMMAND: **stty** *[options] [settings]*

> **Objective:** Sets terminal I/O options for the current standard input device.
>
> **Options & Variables**
>
> | | |
> |---|---|
> | -a | Shows current settings of the currently logged-in terminal. |
> | -g | Reports current settings in hexadecimal. |
> | *settings* | Settings can be either the output of a previous -g flag or a series of **stty** commands. |

COMMAND: **tail** *[options] [file]*

> **Objective:** Lets you view the last lines of a text file. The default is the last 10 lines.

Options & Variables

+n	Outputs *n* lines from the beginning of the input.
-n	Outputs *n* lines from the end of the input.
b	Refers to clocks when added after +n or -n.
c	Refers to characters when added after +n or -n.
r	Outputs the lines in reverse order.

COMMAND: **tar** *[options]* *[files]*

Objective: Copies *files* to or restores *files* from an archive medium. If any *files* are directories, the whole subtree is acted upon. Options don't need to be preceded by -.

Options & Variables

Function Options:

c	Create a new archive.
r	Appends the *files* to an existing archive file.
t	Prints the names of *files* as they appear in the archive file.
u	Performs an update, appending files to the archive if they're not already present or if they've been modified since the last backup.
x	Extracts specified *files* from an archive.

Options:

A	Suppresses absolute file names.
f *archive*	Store *files* in or extract *files* from the specified *archive*.
l	Print error messages about links that aren't found.
m	Don't restore modification times, update them to the time of extraction.
v	File names are displayed as they're being processed.
w	Wait for user confirmation.

COMMAND: **tee** *[options] files*

Objective: Split the output into two files. Send one copy to standard output, the other to *files*.

Options & Variables

-a	Append output to *files* rather than overwriting them.
-i	Ignores all interrupts.
-u	Causes output to be unbuffered.
files	The space separated list of files into which you want to capture the output.

COMMAND: **time** *command*

> **Objective:** Prints the amount of execution time, process execution time, and system time for a process.
>
> **Options & Variables**
>
> | | |
> |---|---|
> | *command* | The command you want to time. |

COMMAND: **tr** *[options] [string1] [string2]*

> **Objective:** Copies standard input to standard output, substituting characters from *string1* to *string2* or deleting characters in *string1*.
>
> **Options & Variables**
>
> | | |
> |---|---|
> | -c | Restricts the output to the characters specified in *string1* and effectively appends those characters in *string2*. |
> | -d | Delete characters in *string1* from the output. |
> | -s | Strip out repeated output characters in *string2*. |

COMMAND: **unmask** *[value]*

> **Objective:** Displays or sets the file creation mode mask.
>
> **Options & Variables**
>
> | | |
> |---|---|
> | *value* | A three-digit octal code specifying the read-write-execute permissions to be turned off. |

COMMAND: **unpack** *files*

> **Objective:** Expands one or more *files*, created with **pack**, to their original form.

COMMAND: **unset** *[-f] names*

> **Objective:** Erases definitions of variables or functions listed in *names*. In the Korn shell, the functions must be stated explicitly with the -f option.

COMMAND: **wall** *[file]*

> **Objective:** Sends a message to all logged-in users. If a *file* is indicated, input is taken from the file rather than standard input.

COMMAND: **who** *[options]*

> **Objective:** Displays information about the current status of the system. With no options, you'll get a list of currently logged-in users.
>
> **Options & Variables**
>
> | | |
> |---|---|
> | am i | Prints the name of the user invoking the command. |
> | -A | Displays UNIX accounting information. |
> | -a | Shows all available information. |
> | -b | Reports information about the last reboot. |

-H	Prints the header line.
-l	Reports inactive terminal lines.
-q	Displays only the user names and a count.
-t	Reports the last change of the system clock.

COMMAND: **whodo**

Objective: Reports a list of who is on the system and what they're doing.

COMMAND: **write** *user [tty]*

Objective: Lets you send a message to another user's terminal (if they've allowed it through the use of the **mesg** command).

Options & Variables

user	The name of the person to whom you want to send the message.
tty	If the person happens to be logged into more than one terminal, you can specify the terminal you want the message to go to.

COMMAND: **xsetroot** *[options]*

> **Objective:** Sets the appearance of the workspace's background.
>
> ### Options & Variables
>
> | | |
> |---|---|
> | -help | Displays a summary of command-line options. |
> | -def | Resets unspecified attributes to their default settings. |
> | -bitmap *file* | Uses the bitmap found in *file* to set the workspace background. |
> | -mod *x y* | Makes a plaid background. The x and y are integers from 1 to 16. |
> | -gray | Makes a gray background. |
> | -solid *color* | Makes the workspace background a solid *color*. |

COMMAND: **xterm** *[options]*

> **Objective:** Lets you set the windows variables.
>
> ### Options & Variables
>
> | | |
> |---|---|
> | -bg *color* | Sets the background color of the **xterm** window. |
> | -fg *color* | Sets the foregorund to *color*. |
> | -fn *font* | Substitutes *font* for the default font. |
> | -help | Displays a summary of available **xterm** options. |

-RV	Reverses the foreground and background colors.
-sb or +sb	Displays a scroll bar for the **xterm** window and saves lines that are scrolled off the top so they can still be viewed.

COMMAND: **zcat** *file*

Objective: Displays uncompressed output for the contents of a compressed file (one ending with .z) while leaving the compressed file unchanged.

Error Messages

Most of the error messages in UNIX are pretty straightforward. In other words, if you ask to switch to a directory called WORKFIPES and UNIX reports that such a directory doesn't exist, it wouldn't take you long to figure out that you'd mistyped WORKFILES. But some messages are moderately or extremely cryptic, so we're including them in this appendix, in alphabetical order.

-c: bad option(s)

You invoked a shell with an option that the shell didn't understand.

at: bad date specification

The time at which the job is to be executed is stated incorrectly.

bad conversion

The **date** setting syntax is incorrect.

bad format character

You didn't use a valid format character. See the list under the **date** command in Appendix A.

bad string

When using the **tr** command, the two strings are not equal.

cannot open ...

Indicates a problem with the file system. Call the System Administrator.

cannot open item

You've invoked the **news** command to read an article, but the specified article doesn't exist.

can't assign *device*

The device is not in the assignable device table.

cat: input *filename* is output

You used the same file as both an input and an output file.

cmp: EOF on *file*

In doing a compare, one of the files is shorter than the other. The system will substitute the name of the shorter file for *file*.

crontab: can't open your crontab file

Assuming you're authorized to use **cron**, you probably tried to list your **crontab** file using the -l flag or you gave a bad flag and **crontab** interpreted it as a file name.

ERROR: arg counter (bd1)

The wrong number of arguments has been supplied. Probably one of the file names is incorrect.

find: bad option - *the_invalid_stuff*

When using the **find** command, you have to supply a matching specification for the files you want to find. Whatever you supplied isn't valid. *the_invalid_stuff* is replaced with what you specified.

find: incomplete statement

That fussy **find** command is saying that you didn't supply enough arguments.

INVALID OPTION (-*x*) - PROCESSING TERMINATED

This dire-looking message merely means that you gave the **nl** command with an option it doesn't recognize. The system substitutes the option letter you specified for -*x*.

line too long

You're trying to input a line using **cut** or output a line using **paste** that's longer than 511 characters.

ptar: directory checksum error

You may have specified the wrong media type for the floppy or tape drive, or the tape may need to be rewound.

Read error in ...

Indicates a problem with the file system. Call the System Administrator.

rm: illegal option — ?

You supplied **rm** with an option it doesn't recognize.

shutdown: not found

Means that **/etc** is not in your search PATH. It's only in the PATH for the Superuser, so you can't use this command unless you are, in fact, that very important personage.

Sorry

This brief statement of sympathy pops up when you try to change your password and you enter your old password incorrectly. You'll need to invoke **passwd** and try again.

sort: invalid use of command-line options

Notification that you gave **sort** an option it doesn't recognize.

tar: directory checksum error

You may have specified the wrong media type for the floppy or tape drive, or the tape may need to be rewound.

too many files

You're trying to **paste** together more than 12 files.

unknown tab code

When using the **tabs** command with the -*list* option, you've tried to specify a tab stop that doesn't exist.

Where To Go From Here

We use a lot of UNIX resources and we're constantly discovering more. Here we present the ones we've used the most, not only in writing this book, but also in our daily UNIX lives. If you find others, please let us know. We hope you'll find exploring these resources like opening a door into a whole new room of the library that you never knew existed.

Books, Books & More Books

Not surprisingly, we have a preference for *books* as a resource. Here are some of the best we have found.

General UNIX Books

These books are not about one particular feature or flavor of UNIX, but about the subject in general. We have seen many others, but these are the ones we liked the best.

Abrahams, Paul and Bruce R. Larson. *UNIX for the Impatient.* Redding, MA: Addison-Wesley, 1992.

A good starting place if you already know a little and want to learn more. Dense at times, but covers most things at least a bit, and sometimes quite well. Probably not for the raw beginner.

Gilley, Daniel. *UNIX in a Nutshell: A Desktop Quick Referecne for System V & Solaris 2.0. 2nd ed.* Cambridge, MA: O'Reilly & Associates, 1992.

Dense but comprehensive. Covers almost everything with good examples. A valuable reference to have on your desktop.

Nutshell Handbook Editors & Jerry Peek. *UNIX Power Tools.* New York, NY: Bantam, 1993.

Includes a CD-ROM with all sorts of goodies on it. An excellent book for those who are beyond the beginner stage. The organization is a bit difficult to get used to, but it seems to work in the end.

The Waite Group. *UNIX Papers for UNIX Developers & Power Users.* Carmel, IN: Sams, 1987.

We're indebted to Gary Masters for pointing us to this book. It has some excellent topics in it, though it's uneven because it's a collection of papers written by various authors. The paper on shells is excellent.

Vendor-Specific UNIX Books

Many of the books written and oriented toward a specific vendor's implementation of UNIX are nonetheless good general references. Here are some we use:

Cutler, Ellie. *SCO UNIX in a Nutshell.* Cambridge, MA: O'Reilly & Associates, 1994.

The SCO version of the *UNIX in a Nutshell* book. Just as comprehensive, just as dense, still a good book to have on your desk and one of the first we pull out if the man page wasn't quite enough.

Heslop, Brent D. and David Angell. *Mastering Solaris 2*. Alameda, CA: Sybex.

Interesting mostly as an operating system moving from BSD to AT&T style, but has a useful command reference.

Spicer, Peter. *Inside SCO Unix. 2nd ed*. Carmel, IN: New Riders Publishing, 1993.

Has an excellent and easily understood command reference. Generally pretty accessible.

The Korn Shell

Always one of our favorite topics, and a source of both satisfaction and frustration.

Korn, David G. and Morris I. Bolsky. *The Korn Shell Command &Programming Language*. New York, NY: Prentice Hall, 1989.

Written by the guys who should know, this is a good book, though not for beginners.

Rosenberg, Barry. *KornShell Programming Tutorial*. Redding, MA: Addison-Wesley, 1991.

Good coverage of a number of topics. Stronger as a tutorial than as a reference.

Rosenblatt, Bill. *Learning the Korn Shell*. Cambridge, MA: O'Reilly & Associates, 1993.

A good intermediate-level book, with clear explanations. Covers interactive command-line use as well as shell programming.

Valley, John. *UNIX Desktop Guide to the Korn Shell*. Carmel, IN: Sams, 1991.

Seems to be more about the Bourne shell than the Korn shell in places, and covers more general UNIX topics than one would expect in a shell-specific book.

Text Editors

Another favorite subject, and an area where we are constantly looking for new resources.

Cameron, Deb and Bill Rosenblatt. *Learning GNU Emacs*. Cambridge, MA: O'Reilly & Associates, 1991.

A good book for beginning-to-intermediate Emacs users, where most of the books out there seem to be much too dense.

Hewlett-Packard Company Staff. *The Ultimate Guide to the VI and EX*. Redwood City, CA: Benjamin-Cummings Publishing Co., 1990.

We're not sure it's the ultimate guide, but it's certainly a good one. Covers **vi** thoroughly and well.

Lamb, Linda. *Learning the vi Editor*. Cambridge, MA: O'Reilly & Associates, 1991.

A good, comprehensive book. It includes a very useful pull-out quick-reference card we're always fighting over.

Text Processors & Languages

Most of the tasks that one uses **awk,** **sed** and **perl** for can be done by hand, but when you start to do them repeatedly, its time to find a way to beat the tedium.

Aho, Alfred V., et al. *The AWK Programming Language.* Redding, MA: Addison-Wesley, 1988.

Written by the authors of the language, it is comprehensive but not always comprehensible. But an essential reference.

Dougherty, Dale. *sed & awk.* Cambridge, MA: O'Reilly & Associates, 1990.

Dense but excellent coverage that ties these two important resources together.

Schwartz, Randal. *Learning Perl.* Cambridge, MA: O'Reilly & Associates, 1993.

An excellent tutorial coverage of **perl** for the person new to the language.

Wall, Larry and Randal Schwartz. *Programming Perl.* Cambridge, MA: O'Reilly & Associates, 1991.

Too dense by far for the beginner, but an excellent reference once you get going.

The X Window System

Most of the books available cover X for programmers, not users. The two listed here manage to address the rest of us.

Quercia, Valerie and Tim O'Reilly. *X Window System Users Guide. 4th ed. Vol. 3*. Cambridge, MA: O'Reilly & Associates, 1993.

> This is a huge volume, and it's one of an even huger set of books oriented toward the programmer of X. But this one provides a good reference for users. Doesn't cover Motif or OpenLook at all but does cover the twm window manager that comes with X.

Southerton, Alan. *The Shell Hacker's Guide to X &Motif: Custom Power Tools & Window Manager Tricks*. New York, NY: Wiley, 1993.

> Not really much about X—more about how to make Motif jump through some interesting hoops.

Other Books

Probably the single best resource, when you just want a quick answer to something, is the man page on that particular program. Nine times out of ten, this will be all the information you need. If you prefer hard-copy books, however, the UNIX manuals that come with your system are the same man pages, all pulled together into a book. The only problem is, they are probably taking up several feet of space on your System Administrator's desk.

However, if you ask nicely, there are frequently additional copies floating around that you can use. Or you can even order a whole set if you want to be ostentatious about it. But be warned that anyone with official manuals on their desk is likely to end up becoming the next System Administrator. Don't say we didn't warn you.

Online Resources

The vast world of the Internet offers an almost unlimited resource for the UNIX user. But it can be an intimidating place, especially for the person moving to UNIX from a PC. In the commercial online world, there is CompuServe which has several UNIX-related forums. For general UNIX stuff, the UNIX Forum (GO UNIXFORUM at any ! prompt) is excellent, with lots of help and tips. For those using SCO, the SCO Forum (GO SCOFORUM) is outstanding. We found this to be among the very best of the CompuServe forums, and the Libraries have all the latest updates for SCO users, as well as precompiled versions of many popular programs.

For obtaining programs in source code, we were able to find much of what we wanted available for anonymous ftp from ftp.uu.net. Another good source is archive.cis.ohio-state-edu, and for precompiled SCO versions of many programs we're indebted to Bill Campbell and ftp.celestial.com.

Glossary

A

absolute pathname   The complete name of a file, including the total path of directories showing the file's location of the directory tree. An absolute path name starts with the root directory—/.

address   Either the name of a specific machine or the name of the entire UNIX system. Both meanings are used in discussions of email and communications.

AIX   A version of UNIX made by IBM Corporation.

anonymous ftp   A remote login that requires no password. You type in the word anonymous as the user name and your electronic mail address as the password, enabling you to copy files from another computer to your own.

archive   A file containing a collection of other files. Chiefly used for backup.

argument   On a command line, something that follows a command. For example, on a line that reads **cp my.file your.file** the command is **cp**, the **my.file** is the first argument and the **your.file** is the second argument.

ASCII   Stands for American Standard Code for Information Interchange. Usually means a file that's in text, is therefore viewable and printable, and has no binary (non-ASCII) characters.

at   Command that lets you schedule tasks to be run in the future.

awk   A programming language geared toward text manipulation.

B

background   A "place" behind the scenes where a program that needs no input from you runs in the background. Commands can be run in the background by starting them with an ampersand (&) at the end of the command line.

backslash   The character \ which in UNIX changes ("escapes") the interpretation of the next character.

bang   The character ! A shell escape character. Also used to indicate that the command should be carried out regardless.

Berkeley Software Distribution   The long name for BSD UNIX, a version of UNIX, notable for its advanced networking capabilities, that was developed and distributed by the University of California at Berkeley.

bin directory   A directory for storing executable files. Your home directory probably has a subdirectory named bin.

block size   The largest amount of data that a UNIX file system will allocate contiguously. In other words, files that occupy less than the block size will always be contiguous. Larger files may be fragmented.

Bourne shell   The original shell, created by Steven Bourne of Bell Labs. Its program name is **sh** and it prompts with **$**.

BSD   See **Berkeley Software Distribution.**

buffer   A temporary storage area, such as a file or an area of the computer's memory. Lots of things have buffers, including printers and many text editors.

C

C, C++   The programming languages in which virtually all UNIX programs are written. UNIX itself is written mostly in C. C and its enhanced relative, C++, were both developed at Bell Labs and are widely used by UNIX programmers.

C Shell   A shell written to look as much as possible like the C programming language. It prompts you with %. Its program name is **csh**.

client   In the X Window System, an application, as opposed to the server that manages the resources and provides the display. In a distributed file system, a client is a terminal or workstation connected to a server.

command line   The text you type at a shell prompt. A command line can have more than one command separated by an operator such as a semicolon (;), a pipe (|) or double ampersands (&&).

command mode   The mode in which a program expects the input to consist of executable commands.

command substitution   Using the output of one command as input for another command.

compiler   A program that turns source code into an executable program. For example, C programming code must be run through a compiler before the computer can recognize the code as a program.

compression   A way to shrink files so they don't take up as much space. Programs that do this include **compress** and **pack**.

concatenate   To combine two or more sequences of characters into a single sequence.

control character   A character you make by holding down the Ctrl key while pressing another key.

core dump   A quaint phrase describing a memory listing produced when a program terminates abnormally. The term originated decades ago when magnetic cores were used for memory storage.

current directory   The starting point for path names that don't begin with /. A file name by itself is assumed to refer to a file in the current directory. Also called the *working directory*.

current job   The job most recently started or stopped. When you use the **jobs** command to see a list of jobs, the current job will be marked with a plus sign (+).

D

daemon   (Pronounced "demon.") A program that's invisible to users but works in the background performing important housekeeping tasks. Daemons manage everything from networking to printing to notifying you of incoming mail. (Now if we could just find one that does dishes!)

default   A value or state assumed when no other is supplied.

dot (.) files   Files that are read when you log in. If you use the C shell, it will read **.cshrc** and **.login**. Bourne shell reads **.profile**. Korn shell uses **.profile** and **.kshrc.** Dot files set up your environment and are "hidden" from the ordinary **ls** command.

double quote   The " character. The " is used around a UNIX command to instruct the shell to do variable and command substitution but no other interpretation. See also **single quote.**

dumb terminal   A terminal that has no processing power of its own. It usually doesn't have any nice stuff like a mouse or a screen that can do graphics either.

E

end of file (EOF) character   The character that indicates the end of a file. In UNIX, it's the combination Crtl-D.

environment variable   A shell setting that makes up part of your environment. For example, one environment variable can be the designation of a particular directory as your HOME directory.

escape   A character, usually a backslash or a tilde, that gives a special meaning to the character or characters that follow it.

etc   Directory containing everything but device files and program files.

execute permission   A setting for an executable file that denotes who can run the program.

F

file system   A set of files stored on a disk or one partition of a disk. A system has one root file system containing files and subdirectories and may have additional file systems mounted on it. Each file system contains files and subdirectories that in turn may contain further subdirectories. Any directory can hold files.

filter   A type of UNIX program that takes input from one file and provides output to the display or another file. The **more** and **sort** commands are commonly used filters.

foreground   A program that has control of your terminal. In UNIX, the default is to run commands in the foreground.

fork   A child process that UNIX creates when it starts a new process. The process is called *forking*.

ftp   (Stands for File Transfer Protocol.) A protocol that defines how to transfer files from one computer to another. It's most often used to describe a program that moves files using the File Transfer Protocol.

G

gateway A computer that connects two or more networks and relays messages and other communications from one network to another.

globbing The Berkeley Term for *file substitution*.

GNU (Gnu's Not Unix) A system of software to eventually become a freely available substitute for UNIX. Developed by the Free Software Foundation, 675 Massachusetts Avenue, Cambridge, MA 02139.

gravè The character ` that's used for command substitution. Also called a *prime*. Not the same as a single quote (').

H

header The first part of an electronic mail message that gives information about the message, such as the sender's name and when it was delivered. Can also refer to a descriptive block of information at the beginning of an archive file.

hidden file A file beginning with a dot (**.login**, for example) that's not normally returned by the **ls** command.

history A record of previous commands maintained in the computer's memory. Only in the C and Korn shells.

HOME The environment variable containing the full path name of your home directory.

home directory The directory the user is deposited in after logging in. This is set with the HOME= command in the **.profile** file.

host A computer that provides services to other computers.

hostname The name of your UNIX system.

I

I/O Input and output. Information going into or coming out of a computer or program.

inode Pronounced "eye-node," it's short for information node. A data structure that describes a file—where the file is stored, how long it is, and so forth. In any file system, the number of inodes, and therefore the maximum number of files, is set when the file system is created.

input mode The mode in which a text editor accepts input and includes it in the edited file. Input mode is the opposite of command mode.

J

job The contents of one command line, no matter how complex. For example, **cat perl.tar.Z | zcat | tar xvf** is one command line, hence one job, even though it's formed from three processes. This is the definition used in most UNIX documentation, though real people tend to use the terms *job, process,* and *program* interchangeably.

job control Changing the status of a job. This includes starting, stopping, killing and moving between the foreground and the background.

job shell   A superset of the Bourne shell that's devoted to job control.

K

kernel   The core of the operating system that interacts directly with the computer. The *kernel* allocates resources, maintains the file system and manages the computer's memory.

kill character   The character that when typed causes the current line to be deleted.

kludge   Rhymes with "huge." A program or a feature that doesn't work as well as it should or gives the impression of being jerry-rigged. Not something the programmer is especially proud of.

Korn shell   An enhanced version of the Bourne shell written by David Korn. Its program name is **ksh.** It prompts with **$.**

L

library   A set of commonly used C language functions.

link   An entry in a directory, consisting of a file identifier that names a file in the directory and an *inode* number.

login file   See **dot (.) files.**

login name   The name you use when logging in to a UNIX system.

login shell   The shell that's called on your behalf when you log in.

logging in   The process of making a connection to a UNIX machine.

M

mailbox   A file where messages are stored by a mailer.

mailer   A program for sending and receiving electronic mail.

manpage   A file of information about a UNIX command. The **man** command displays detailed technical information about all UNIX commands.

meta key   A specified key used with other keys to create additional key combinations. On a PC keyboard **Alt** is the *meta key*.

metacharacter   A character used in a regular expression or in a shell command that has a special meaning rather than standing for itself. For example, > is a *metacharacter* in a shell command that stands for output redirection.

Motif   A graphical user interface created by the Open Software Foundation and based on the X Window System.

mount   To make a file system available to users either locally or remotely.

N

named pipe   A kind of file that behaves like a *pipe* (see **pipe**) and exists independently of any process. Many different processes can read from it and write to it.

newline   The character that marks the end of a line in most UNIX files. You can usually produce a *newline* at your terminal by pressing either the Enter key or Ctrl-J.

null character   The character whose binary representation is all zeroes. By convention, it's used to mark the end of a string.

NFS   (Network File System) Software that allows UNIX and many non-UNIX systems to share files and printers via a TCP/IP network in a way that makes them appear local to the user.

O

option   An indicator that can be attached to a command to modify what the command does. An option usually begins with a dash (-). The terms *option* and *switch* are more or less interchangeable. An option can have several settings while a switch usually has two: on and off, enabled and disabled.

ordinary file   A text or data file with no special characteristics. The most common type of file in the UNIX system.

orphan   A process that keeps running even when its parent process has been killed.

P

packet   A portion of a message that's transmitted as a unit over a network.

pager   A program that breaks its input into screen-size chunks and sends these pieces to your terminal, waiting for confirmation after each one.

parameter   A variable in the shell script that corresponds to an argument passed to the script.

parent process   A process that generates another process.

parse   To split into pieces to interpret.

permissions   A security tool that controls who can access or change a file.

pipe   A connection between two processes that passes the output of the first to the input of the second. Signified by the pipe (|) character.

pipeline   A sequence of processes connected by *pipes*.

process   A single stream of computer instructions. One *job* may be built from several different *processes*.

.profile   See **dot (.) files**.

prime   Another name for the accent *gravè*.

prompt   A character used by the shell to show that it's waiting for input. In addition, some programs provide their own unique prompts.

Q

quote See **double quote, gravè, single quote**.

queue A waiting line, the most common variety of which is the printing *queue*. (Also the only English word with five vowels in a row without a consonant.)

R

real-time Right now as opposed to whenever the computer gets around to it.

recursive A program or routine that repeats an action over and over. For example, the **find** program moves through a directory tree *recursively*, doing something in every directory.

redirection Taking the output of a command and sending it somewhere other than the default location.

regular expression An expression used to specify a set of *strings* being searched for. Regular expressions use *metacharacters* to specify variables.

reset string A *string* that can be sent to a crazy, mixed-up terminal, restoring it to sanity.

root Another name for the Superuser.

root directory The main, top-level directory of a file system. All the files in the system are either in the *root directory* or in a subdirectory of the root directory (or a subdirectory of a subdirectory, and so on).

S

server   In a distributed file system, a computer that supplies files and services to other computers.

shell   A program that reads and interprets commands from the user into instructions the computer can understand. Popular shells include the Bourne, Korn and C shells.

shell script   A file that contains a list of UNIX shell commands. When you run a shell script you're telling UNIX to execute every command in the list.

single quote   The ' character. This is not the same as the *gravè* (`). The single quote is used around the part of the command line where the shell should do no interpretation.

slash   The / character. It separates elements in a pathname. See also **backslash**.

string   A sequence of characters.

Superuser   The person logged in under the name *root* who has permission to access any file and carry out other operations not permitted to mere mortals.

swapping   Using the hard disk as temporary storage when RAM is at a premium.

switch   See **option**.

System Administrator   The person responsible for keeping the UNIX system running smoothly and securely.

T

TCP/IP (Transport Control Protocol/Internet Protocol) A network protocol used to link UNIX and non-UNIX computers worldwide over a wide variety of media, from high-speed optical network cabling to regular phone lines.

terminal A screen and keyboard connected to a computer located somewhere else.

terminal emulator A program that enables a big, powerful computer to act like a small, dumb one. Typically, a PC can run a terminal emulator so you can use another computer running UNIX.

timestamp UNIX stores the time when a file was last modified, accessed or had a change to its inode. These times—especially the time of modification—are called *timestamps*.

toggle To turn features on or off.

truncate To cut or shorten. For example the instruction to truncate a file after line 20 means to remove all lines after line 20.

U–V

UUCP (UNIX-to-UNIX System Copy) Program that copies files from one system to another over ordinary phone lines.

vi A very powerful text editor that's packaged with most UNIX systems.

W

window manager   An X window program that defines how other programs appear and behave on the screen.

working directory   The directory you're currently in. The **pwd** command identifies your working directory.

X

X server   A program that draws the screen display if you use the X Window System or one of its relatives.

X terminal   A terminal that can act as an X server but relies on a machine elsewhere on the network for most of its computing power.

X Window System   A graphical windowing system developed by MIT that's the basis for fuller interfaces such as Motif or OPEN LOOK.

xterm   A popular X Window program that provides a command-line interface to the UNIX operating system.

Index

COLOPHON

Voodoo UNIX was produced on a Macintosh Quadra 700, using PageMaker 5.0. Body text is set in Digital Typeface Corporation (DTC) Galliard Roman, tip and trap names are DTC Classical Sans Bold Condensed, running heads and folios are DTC Classical Sans Bold, subheads and chapter titles are Adobe Caxton Bold and sidebars are set in DTC Classical Sans Condensed. Screen shots were created using pbmplus (freeware) and xv (shareware).

NOTES

NOTES

NOTES

NOTES

NOTES

Ventana Companions

Windows, Word & Excel
Office Companion, Second Edition
$21.95
544 pages, illustrated
ISBN: 1-56604-083-3
Your Microsoft business bible. This three-in-one reference is organized as a quick course in each program. Chapters contain valuable information on basic commands and features, plus helpful tutorials, tips and shortcuts.

Voodoo Windows
$19.95
282 pages, illustrated
ISBN: 1-56604-005-1
A unique resource, *Voodoo Windows* bypasses the technical information found in many Windows books to bring you an abundance of never-before-published tips, tricks and shortcuts for maximum Windows productivity. A one-of-a-kind reference for beginners and experienced users alike.

The Windows Shareware 500
$39.95
417 pages, illustrated, 4 disks
ISBN: 1-56604-045-0
This value-packed book/disk set introduces the world of affordable software. Comes with 4 disks, including America Online membership disks and 10 hours of free online time.

To order any Ventana Press title, use the form in the back of this book or contact your local bookstore or computer store.

For Creative Computing

Desktop Publishing With WordPerfect 6 for Windows

$24.95
261 pages, illustrated
ISBN: 1-56604-086-8

A Windows bestseller, WordPerfect 6.0's vastly improved graphics tools and features can save you thousands of dollars in design and typesetting costs. Includes invaluable design advice and annotated examples.

Word for Windows Design Companion, Second Edition

$21.95
504 pages, illustrated
ISBN: 1-56604-075-2

Learn the basics of good design with step-by-step instructions. Filled with innovative design advice and creative examples for getting the most from your Word investment. Covers Word for Windows through Version 6.

Desktop Publishing With Word for Windows, Second Edition

$21.95
352 pages, illustrated
ISBN: 1-56604-074-4

Desktop Publishing With Word for Windows, Second Edition, is your key to creating attractive newsletters, brochures, ads, proposals and reports, correspondence and more with Microsoft Word.

Immediate shipment guaranteed
Full money-back guarantee

Design and

Advertising From the Desktop
$24.95
427 pages, illustrated
ISBN: 1-56604-064-7
Advertising From the Desktop offers unmatched design advice and helpful how-to instructions for creating persuasive ads. With tips on how to choose fonts, select illustrations, apply special effects and more, this book is an idea-packed resource for improving the looks and effects of your ads.

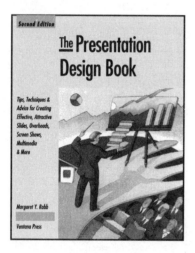

The Presentation Design Book, Second Edition
$24.95
320 pages, illustrated
ISBN: 1-56604-014-0
The Presentation Design Book is filled with thoughtful advice and instructive examples for creating business presentation visuals, including charts, overheads, type, etc., that help you communicate and persuade. The *Second Edition* adds advice on the use of multimedia. For use with any software or hardware.

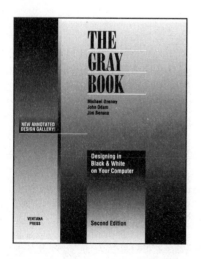

The Gray Book, Second Edition
$24.95
262 pages, illustrated
ISBN: 1-56604-073-6
This "idea gallery" for desktop publishers offers a lavish variety of the most interesting black, white and gray graphic effects that can be achieved with laser printers, scanners and high-resolution output devices. The *Second Edition* features new illustrations, synopses and steps, added tips and an updated appendix.

Conquer

Looking Good in Print, Third Edition
$24.95
412 pages, illustrated
ISBN: 1-56604-047-7
For use with any software or hardware, this desktop design bible has become the standard among novice and experienced desktop publishers alike. With over 200,000 copies in print, *Looking Good in Print* is even better, with new sections on photography and scanning.

The Makeover Book: 101 Design Solutions for Desktop Publishing
$17.95
282 pages, illustrated
ISBN: 0-940087-20-0
Transform your work from average to outstanding! Seeing original "before-and-after" desktop publishing examples, you'll learn how basic design principles can dramatically improve your ads, brochures, flyers and more.

Newsletters From the Desktop
$23.95
306 pages, illustrated
ISBN: 0-940087-40-5
Now the millions of desktop publishers who produce newsletters can learn how to improve the design of their publications. Filled with helpful design tips and illustrations.

Can't wait? Call toll-free:
800/743-5369 *(U.S. only)*

At Last, the Internet Puts on a Friendly Face!

On the Internet, there's a hard way and an easy way to do almost anything. The Internet is often a maze of obscure commands and error messages. But *The Internet Tour Guides* get you up to cruising speed so you can explore the infinite reaches of the electronic highway— the easy way!

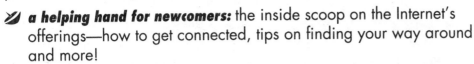

To order any Ventana Press title, fill out this order form and mail it to us with payment for quick shipment.

	Quantity		Price		Total
Advertising *From the Desktop*	_____	x	$24.95	=	$ _____
The Official America Online for Windows Membership Kit & Tour Guide	_____	x	34.95	=	$ _____
Desktop Publishing With Word for Windows, 2nd Edition	_____	x	$21.95	=	$ _____
Desktop Publishing With WordPerfect 6 for Windows	_____	x	$24.95	=	$ _____
The Gray Book, 2nd Edition	_____	x	$24.95	=	$ _____
Looking Good in Print, 3rd Edition	_____	x	$24.95	=	$ _____
The Mac Internet Tour Guide	_____	x	$27.95	=	$ _____
The Makeover Book	_____	x	$17.95	=	$ _____
Newsletters From the Desktop	_____	x	$24.95	=	$ _____
The PC Internet Tour Guide	_____	x	$24.95	=	$ _____
The Presentation Design Book, 2nd Edition	_____	x	$24.95	=	$ _____
Voodoo UNIX	_____	x	$27.95	=	$ _____
Voodoo Windows	_____	x	$19.95	=	$ _____
The Windows Internet Tour Guide	_____	x	$24.95	=	$ _____
The Windows Shareware 500	_____	x	$39.95	=	$ _____
Windows, Word & Excel Office Companion, 2nd Edition	_____	x	$21.95	=	$ _____
Word for Windows Design Companion, 2nd Edition	_____	x	$21.95	=	$ _____
			Subtotal	=	$ _____

SHIPPING:
For all regular orders, please <u>add</u> $4.50/first book, $1.35/each additional.　　= $ _____
For "two-day air," <u>add</u> $8.25/first book, $2.25/each additional.　　= $ _____
For orders to Canada, <u>add</u> $6.50/book.　　= $ _____
For orders sent C.O.D., <u>add</u> $4.50 to your shipping rate.　　= $ _____
North Carolina residents must <u>add</u> 6% sales tax.　　= $ _____
　　TOTAL = $ _____

Name _____ Company _____

Address (No PO Box) _____

City _____ State _____ Zip _____

Daytime Telephone _____ ___ Payment enclosed ___VISA ___MC

Acc't # _____ Expiration Date _____

Signature _____

Mail or fax to: Ventana Press, PO Box 2468, Chapel Hill, NC 27515 ☎ 919/942-0220 Fax 919/942-1140
International Customers: Write or fax us at above address for information on our distributors worldwide.

CAN'T WAIT? CALL TOLL-FREE ☎ 800/743-5369 (U.S. only)